All Mothers Work

VIRGINIA TAPSCOTT

Published in Australia by
Halcyon Publishing
PO Box 88, Church Point, NSW 2105

First published in Australia 2025
Copyright © Virginia Tapscott 2025

All rights reserved. No part of this publication may be reproduced, stored in a retrieval system, or transmitted, in any form or by any means without the prior written permission of the publisher, nor be otherwise circulated in any form of binding or cover other than that in which it is published and without a similar condition being imposed on the subsequent purchaser.

National Library of Australia Cataloguing in Publication entry

 A catalogue record for this book is available from the National Library of Australia

ISBN: 978-1-7640430-3-8 (paperback)
ISBN: 978-1-7640430-1-4 (hardcover)
ISBN: 978-1-7640430-2-1 (epub)

Cover design by Senophia
Book layout and design by Sophie White Design

Printed by Kindle Direct Publishing

All care has been taken in the preparation of the information herein, but no responsibility can be accepted by the publisher or author for any damages resulting from the misinterpretation of this work. All contact details given in this book were current at the time of publication, but are subject to change.

The advice given in this book is based on the experience of the individuals. Professionals should be consulted for individual problems. The author and publisher shall not be responsible for any person with regard to any loss or damage caused directly or indirectly by the information in this book.

ALL MOTHERS WORK

A Revolutionary Plan to Fix Failing Care Systems and Truly Liberate Women

VIRGINIA TAPSCOTT

For Mum, who taught me the value of care.

Parents Work Collective is a not-for-profit advocacy group working to increase support for parents. Alannah Batho and Virginia Tapscott co-founded PWC in 2022 after becoming frustrated with the lack of support for parents in their capacity as caregivers. They seek to challenge government policy that persistently incentivises a return to work, often at the expense of children's and parents' wellbeing. PWC aims to increase measures that support vital care work and create genuine choices for families in how they care for their children. Ultimately, PWC defends a parent's right to care for their young children at home in the earliest years.

PWC has made submissions to a string of government inquiries in recent years, appeared at a Productivity Commission hearing and engaged the media on many family related issues. It has also appeared at international conferences. PWC's website and Instagram page have also attracted a significant online following consisting of parents who share the frustrations with existing policy.

All proceeds from sales of the book will go to Parents Work Collective to support ongoing advocacy work.

hello@parentsworkcollective.org.au
www.parentsworkcollective.org.au
Instagram: @parentsworkcollective
LinkedIn: Parents Work Collective

Contents

Chapter One	The Mother of All	11
Chapter Two	Women Aren't the Problem	22
Chapter Three	Since the Apes Started Walking	38
Chapter Four	Care is Real Work	49
Chapter Five	Valuing Care Work	63
	Everyday language	*63*
	'Stay-at-home mum' versus 'working mum'	*67*
	Baby brain	*71*
	Misplaced misery	*75*
	Valuing paid care work, too	*76*
	Tradwife saga	*77*
	Shifting our internalised beliefs	*81*
	Value of caregiving reflected in society	*84*
Chapter Six	Pregnancy and Postpartum	86
Chapter Seven	An Extra Set of Hands	107
Chapter Eight	Giving Parents Time to Parent	116
Chapter Nine	Welcome to the World of Daycare Research	127
Chapter Ten	What Can Daycare Research Tell Us?	143
Chapter Eleven	The Business of Raising Kids	166
Chapter Twelve	Rebuilding the Village	180
Chapter Thirteen	Reclaiming Care from Capitalism	189
Chapter Fourteen	The Money Problem	204
	Living rurally	*214*
	Work flexibility	*215*
	Cutting back spending	*215*
	Delayed home buying	*215*
Chapter Fifteen	The End of Elitist Feminism	223
Chapter Sixteen	Conclusion	234
Endnotes		238
About the Author		251
Author Contact		251
Acknowledgements		252

CHAPTER ONE

The Mother of All

The cry of my first-born drove me mad. I could not stand the sound of it. Every time he started up, it was like an electric shock jolted right through me. I felt extremely agitated until I was holding him and actively trying to make it stop. Under a set of less fortunate circumstances—without a supportive partner or without trusted, unwavering family and friends, perhaps without financial security—there is no telling what might have been in those early months of motherhood for me. I know how easily things could have spiralled.

There is a liminal space between reality and madness. Some of us get to that space and have someone or something that can help us back out. Some of us slip right in. Motherhood is an extraordinary psychological transformation and with that comes opportunity for growth but also risks. I think it's because of motherhood that I have danced closer to the borders of reality than I am comfortable with. It can be a strange kind of portal to the best and the worst in us. An extraordinary catalyst for change dropped into our lives like an effervescent pill into a glass of water. We are fizzing away becoming someone new while fighting to stay the same. I'm stronger now because of this. I know how to spot the mirage where reality bleeds into the unknown – the paranoia, the feeling of being close to the edge. I can see it from a mile off.

The crying that nearly brought me undone had a clear and crucial purpose – it made a mother out of me. There is no other noise on the planet that has ever compelled me into action so instantly and so consistently. In the beginning, I was annoyed on two fronts: he cried a lot so I was often agitated; but also, the effect of his cry meant I wasn't in control. It didn't matter what I was doing; if I heard him so much as squeak or cough, I was there in an instant, peering into the pram or cot. Wild eyed and prepared to leap into action. My body was perpetually ready for the lions that would never come.

By the time I had my fourth baby, having been trained expertly by the cries of the previous three, I was acting almost completely on instinct. In some ways, I was nothing more than a fancy, mostly hairless monkey. Absolutely animal in the way I carried him around with me and tucked him in beside me to sleep. If that child so much as coughed, he had a nipple in his mouth. He had nothing to cry about. I picked him up and I fed him. I accepted fully what needed to be done.

Perhaps, had I been more conditioned to the reality of motherhood, more exposed to its inner workings and familiar with what it involved, the process of becoming a mother may have been less of a shock. Who knew you had to feed a newborn eight-12 times a day? Who knew they wanted to be held constantly? Who knew the nappy changes were relentless?

Not even modern humans, with our university degrees and our fancy technology, shiny implements and gas-fired cooktops, are immune to the wiles of Nature. She will go to great lengths to ensure the survival of a species. My biggest mistake was the war I waged on these age-old biological processes. I mounted a fruitless resistance to a connection far stronger and deeper than for which I was prepared. We cannot ignore, abandon, or even suppress the mother-infant bond without serious and lasting consequences. Mothers and babies do not suddenly evolve out of this ancient dynamic. We know this in our hearts but modern science is also fast unearthing proof.

Neuroscientists now understand in astonishing detail how a mother's brain starts changing from the moment she becomes pregnant in order to better equip her for caregiving. We also understand how our emotional brain-circuits develop in response to caregiving, or specifically, in response to mothering. It's important to remember that 'mother' is as much a verb as it is a noun, as Angela Garbes reminds us in her work: 'Mothering is sensual – endemic to the body and bringing both profound joy and fulfillment,' she writes in *Like a Mother*. 'It cultivates and nurtures a child's life force and essence. It is labour that can bestow a primal sense of satisfaction to children and caregivers alike.'

Acts of mothering are sacred, essential, and often carried out by a range of figures in an infant's life. How we are mothered literally shapes our brain. Research in this area exploded in 2001 when Yale University researchers worked out how to scan healthy infants and toddlers in MRI machines that required them to be perfectly still[1]. Instead of using sedation, which muted brain activity somewhat and posed ethical problems, the researchers scanned babies in natural sleep. In doing so, they flung open the doors on a whole field of unexplored research territory. We could now timestamp brain development in the earliest months and years to work out which parts of the brain were firing up and when. We could trace that brain development right up to adulthood and link the earliest neural changes to later mental illness.

Then came more sophisticated and faster hormone testing – a window into the biochemical processes that built our brains. When hormone testing first became a routine lab experiment in the 1970s, it could take five business days to report results. We now have technologies that can measure the tiniest amounts of oxytocin or cortisol in saliva samples within minutes. We are on the verge of using biosensors to track hormone levels in real time.

While the likes of Bowlby and Freud theorised extensively about the importance and long-term ramifications of the mother-infant bond, it's really only been since the turn of the millennium that we could prove the mechanism for the impact care has on our brain development. We are going beyond the studies of observation that attachment theory was built on. We are measuring the levels of oxytocin or stress hormones flowing through a baby or toddler's body when they are interacting with caregivers. Then being able to see their brain.

In recent decades, we have made discoveries that pose huge ethical and logistical problems for the gender-equality movement as we know it. We now know that mothers tend to elicit higher levels of oxytocin in infants than fathers during affectionate contact, and that fathers tend to elicit higher levels of oxytocin in infants during stimulating interactions like play[2]. We also know that secreting healthy hormone levels during the developmental years is crucial for life long mental and physical health[3]. While this evidence has at times been used to argue the interchangeability of mothers and fathers, it actually reinforces the prominence of mothers in the early months and years thus presenting a problem for equality movements that call for arbitrary, split-down-the-middle-equally division of care labour from birth.

Interactions with infants and toddlers tend to be more about nurturing than play in the beginning. Play and higher stimulation interactions increase as the baby grows into toddlerhood and preschool age, meaning dads can excel in support roles in the early months but are not interchangeable with mothers. So, even though fathers may be perfectly capable of affection and nurture, their biochemistry means they simply do not elicit the same highs in oxytocin as mothers during these earlier interactions.

While researchers had been using neuroimaging technology for decades to unravel the mysteries of adult brains, it has been only in very recent years that infant brains have come under the microscope, and largely since the 2000s that we began studying longitudinal cohorts[4]. Perhaps the most surprising finding has been that the emotional brain circuitry of infants is far more advanced and sensitive than initially thought. 'We know that brain circuits for mood, depression, anxiety, addiction and resilience are all built between conception and age three and last for life,' writes Canadian neuroscientist Greer Kirshenbaum in her book *The Nurture Revolution*. 'After three years of age the most frequently used brain circuits are covered in protective cells and the circuits that were not used frequently are eliminated by pruning.'

Neuroimaging and biochemistry advancements unlocked areas of genetics, epigenetics, psychology and behavioural science that had been hidden until recently. The lasting effects of early-life care became clear. While our emotional brain is influenced by genetics and continues to develop into early adulthood, the foundations of emotional health are laid by our earliest experiences and relationships. We know that in chronic states of prenatal and infancy stress, the brain develops abnormally. In 2019, researchers from the Infant Brain Imaging Study (IBIS) Network demonstrated that the amygdala—the part of the brain that identifies threats and controls emotional processes—had started to overgrow at six months of age in children who would later be diagnosed with neurodevelopmental disorders. Follow-up studies found the babies with faster and earlier amygdala growth were also more likely to have heightened anxiety at school age.

Frustratingly, the study only compared samples of typically developing children with those with high- or low-familial likelihood of developing ASD, presumably to establish more of a genetic basis for conditions like autism. Family history of ASD was not found to be a strong predictor of abnormal amygdala growth, while maternal prenatal depression was associated with overgrown amygdalas. The study did not measure quality of caregiving or environmental stress; however, stress hormones are known to cross the placenta and influence neurodevelopment[5].

Since the amygdala is known to play a key role in triggering the 'flight or fight' response, we can assume that this part of the brain would become enlarged in infants who are exposed to more stress hormones and thus develop a more active stress response. Enlarged amygdalas make sense from an evolutionary perspective, with infants of mothers in more stressful environments primed to develop heightened sensory and visual awareness in order to have a better chance of attracting a caregiver's attention and securing a safe environment.

In the 1990s, researchers began uncovering the relationship between genes that determine our dopamine receptivity—how much of the feel-good hormone we can access—and groups of children characterised as either ultrasensitive or resilient. Professor of paediatrics and psychiatry at the University of California, Dr Thomas Boyce, brought into the mainstream the theory that around 80% of all children were born 'dandelions' with genes that increased dopamine receptivity and therefore made them more resilient to stress. Boyce found the remaining children carried a gene variation that rendered them less receptive to dopamine and categorised them as 'orchids' for their ultra-sensitivity to growing conditions. Orchids can flourish beautifully in ideal conditions or be acutely affected by poor conditions.

High-quality care and reliable early relationships have been found to mitigate the orchid effect. Kirshenbaum explains nurturing care as a crucial way of 'turning the volume down' on genes less favourable to psychological resilience. Nonetheless, orchid children are more sensitive to over-exposure to stress in infancy and face a greater likelihood of their brain being more hypersensitive to stress later in life. Stress is at the seat of the development of all mental illnesses because it interferes with normal brain development and the naturally resilient emotional circuits that come with it.

Given these foundational associations with mothers as a source of comfort or stress, it becomes easy to see how the mother figure has become so deeply ingrained in our psyche, our culture, our art. We orbit around her. As editor of *Quillette*, Claire Lehmann, notes in one of her editorials: 'The Louvre houses over 100 paintings titled "Virgin and Child"'. In 'La Belle Jardiniere', a famous depiction of Mother Mary and Baby Jesus in an informal garden setting, Lehmann notes how the artist, Raphael, 'elevates the maternal to something transcendent … the simple unspoken bond between mother and child'. The beauty of this ordinary moment is inspired not only by religious faith but a deep affinity with the mother figure.

What starts out as an instinctive yearning for her becomes a deep, emotional attachment and later, a fondness, nostalgia, trauma, or all of the above. For better or for worse, and in ways we may never recognise, she shapes our being. Ever the muse of philosophers, academics, poets and screenwriters – the mother figure is central to how we make sense of the world. The word 'mother' itself is synonymous with true origin. It is used to convey all-consuming, ever-guiding, enormity. Mothership, motherlode, motherland. The mother of all.

The dominance of the mother as a fixture in our minds posed a problem for equality movements that sought to equalise workforce participation and early-years caregiving roles in an arbitrary fashion. They had long argued that the mother figure was a cultural construct, a harmful gender stereotype for which there was no biological or evolutionary basis. As ridiculous as this seems, given the obvious differences in male and female biology that necessitates different roles of mothers and fathers, these gender-equality movements were extraordinarily successful in 'playing down' the role of the mother. In the absence of hard evidence such as brain imaging and immunoassays that tracked hormone levels, cultural determinism flourished as a movement that would underpin most forms of feminism.

We have to understand that first-, second-, and part of third-wave feminism occurred in a context where the ideological concepts could not be challenged by science to any large degree. The understanding of male and female biological differences at a microscopic or biochemical level was rudimentary at best. Modern-day workplaces, healthcare, education systems, childcare and parenting culture, much of which remain similar to the present day, were developed at a time when child psychology and the influence of caregiving practices was poorly understood. Political and business movements that sought to deliver childcare at scale and from infancy were well underway, in some cases entrenched, before the research was available. We know better now, but we are so deeply invested in these systems and have structured society around them that we now find ourselves stuck. We see no way out even though we understand, at a scientific level, the ways they are hampering human development. We see no other option but to justify these systems and continue to downplay the mother in service of ideological beliefs and economic systems that require her erasure.

The flaws of the cultural determinism and the feminism they had so believed in would become obvious to each individual woman as she became a mother or eventually realised the inherent differences in the male and female experience. But her individual realisation alone, in the context of broad and powerful social movements, entrenched political views and macro-economic conditions that trapped families into dual-income lifestyles, would not be enough. In motherhood, she was rendered invisible and disempowered by the very movement that had, as a young woman, given her all the opportunities as a man. She couldn't articulate where exactly it all went wrong, and then had no time or energy to come up with solutions. Before long, her children grew out of their dependency and it became a problem for the next woman.

As one of the most determined and intelligent women I have met on this journey put it, "What happens when your matrescence gives you clarity and the world doesn't match?" It's too late. Mothers survive the period where their lived experience is in direct misalignment with their ideological beliefs, they minimise this period by having fewer children, and then they move on. But the problem remains.

The cultural iterations of the mother figure remain, not as a hangover from a backward civilisation but as a seed of truth. Mother Earth. Mother Mary. Mother and child. The mother is impossible to disentangle from our definition of love and the self – our humanity. The mother extends beyond culture and politics; she is a bodily experience we cannot shake no matter how we try.

Fast forward to 2023, and a sports commentator is hauled over the coals for mentioning that one of the athletes on the field is a mother who has returned to elite level following the birth of her daughter two years earlier[6]. Following a tackle by Matilda's midfielder Katrina Gorry, David Basheer commented, "Certainly motherhood has not blunted her competitive instincts, that's for sure."

The criticism levelled at Basheer was not about the infantilising suggestion that motherhood would blunt competitive instincts, but that he mentioned she was a mother at all. Many felt that because the same comment wouldn't be made about a father, it shouldn't have been mentioned. This is where equality becomes erasure. A mother returning to elite soccer fewer than two years after giving birth isn't just noteworthy, it's impossible to ignore. It's an incredible physical feat that no man will ever lay claim to. The comment was in good faith, it was intended as a compliment, but incessant attempts to divorce the mother from the woman mean the mention of motherhood is now a dangerous space.

It seems that these days it is more 'politically correct' to completely omit or ignore motherhood as part of a woman's identity. It's becoming the unsayable. A disturbing example of the steady erasure of motherhood in society and the minimisation of physical and psychological changes that go with it.

If I'm being completely honest with myself, motherhood does have the propensity to make us feel less competitive, at least in the short term, because we can become entirely focused on the baby's survival. Being focused on the baby is a successful and beneficial evolutionary adaptation, and not something of which we should be ashamed. We are in a formidable survival mode that dwarfs almost all other pursuits.

Being less interested in competition may be a feeling that lingers or becomes longer term, particularly if we lack support or experience postpartum physical and mental challenges. Childbirth is life altering; kids can change our focus. It's not a weakness, it's testimony to the enormity of the life-change that is bringing another human into the world.

It is therefore also notable that Gorry has been able to reignite her pre-baby mindset and competitiveness. She has done the work mentally and physically to restore her confidence on-field after an experience that can leave our mind and body feeling a little foreign.

In a social and cultural context where the mother-infant relationship and the mother herself is suppressed, the psychological needs remain but are not sufficiently met. We can't help but feel completely compelled by the idea of mothers and any storyline with a mother in it, but we push back against this. We deny the enormity of her because we are ill-equipped to accommodate her. We know we can't be the mother we want to be so we tell ourselves she was never really necessary in the first place. She is a threat to the idea of equality we have been conditioned to expect. What emerges is a love-hate relationship with the mother figure; a collective disorganised attachment to the idea of her. We catch ourselves slipping into motherhood and fight it. The mother is portrayed as a passive being, a loss of identity, and the lesser.

This book is an effort to counteract the cultural and political forces that have left mothers unsupported and invisible in their work as mothers. What started out as a bid to improve our lives is having perverse and serious impacts that are driving a global health crisis and perpetuating inequality. In this book, we build a new paradigm that does not treat women, motherhood, and caregiving as the problem in the equation but scrutinises the social, ideological, and political context in which they operate. In this book, we will chart the course to promoting equality, better supporting mothers, and adequately meeting the developmental needs of babies and young children.

CHAPTER TWO

Women Aren't the Problem

In recent decades, the lives of women have been held up to the light and forensically inspected. How many hours we work, what we look like, the kind of jobs we end up in, how many kids we have, how much housework we do. These details of our lives and our choices are often illustrated in graphs on the daily news, privately mulled over, publicly debated, and referenced in research. Women have been positioned as a problem to be solved.

Like hamsters on a wheel, we go around and around, running faster, trying harder and doing more to solve the problem we have been made out to be. We hide our pregnancies at work, ignore our bodies, increase our paid work and earn money like never before. Still, the debate rages on – why aren't women working *more*? Why are they so stressed? Why aren't they having *more* kids? The same discussions are dissected and approached from every angle, but the answers elude us... for we are asking the wrong question. We have a gross misdiagnosis on our hands – women are not the problem.

The question is not 'How do we fix women?' but rather 'How do we fix the economic, social, and political systems that devalue the contribution of care?' Once we start asking the right questions, when we recognise that women are making vital contributions both in the workplace and at home, we can start shifting attitudes and implementing policies that assign value to the whole spectrum of women's work.

Rather than address the complexity and enormity of this problem, the way women are inherently disadvantaged in our current structures by their reproductive and care contributions, we decided to minimise the disadvantage simply by enabling women to emulate the linear career progressions of men. Women were a variable that could be controlled more easily and who were more malleable than existing power structures embedded in capitalist economies. We attempted to fix the inherent disadvantages of being a woman by minimising their reproductive and unpaid labour contributions. We set about moulding women into the image of a man.

In recent decades, we have watched on as women have struggled to fit into a paid workplace that wasn't designed for them. The economic empowerment was enormous, but it was a hollow victory because women can never be truly free while equality is conditional. Our mission to liberate women was fundamentally flawed. We can be no closer to addressing the root causes of inequality as long as policies and cultural expectations continue to be guided by the misdiagnosis of women as the problem.

If the real problem is our failure to adequately value care work, our failure to recognise the profound implications care work has for societal functioning, human health, and global economies, then we must trace our way back to the origins of humans to understand how this came to be. We must understand the root causes and the origins of gender inequality and the devaluation of care in order to properly address them. How did women and their work come to be considered inherently inferior? Were women always considered lesser and therefore their contributions always less valuable? How has care work been viewed and supported in societies throughout the ages?

While it is impossible to know for sure how Stone-Age social dynamics played out, archaeological evidence and present-day observation of hunter-gatherer tribes suggests that for some of the earliest humans, reproductive labour and childrearing was as highly valued as any other contribution ranging from procuring food to warfare. The widespread discovery of the Venus Idols—small figurines dating back 10,000 to 35,000 years and depicting what appears to be a pregnant or childbearing-age woman—suggests women and their ability to create life actually increased their status. In some of our earliest known art and ceramics, the dominant creative inspiration, the most powerful muse, was childbirth and the creation of new life. This drove early humans to, quite literally, idolise the pregnant woman or the 'Supreme Creator' as English Professor Helen Benigni argued.

Even with some degree of gendered labour division occurring in tribal settings, and the obvious differences in physical strength between men and women, in the absence of currency there appears to be no logical reason for one contribution to be valued over another. The intelligence and skill required to raise young was just as important to the tribe's existence as those used in defending territory or obtaining food. Everyone needed food and everyone needed to stay alive, but what was the point of their endeavours if there was no one to carry on the evolutionary line?

Physical strength has long been peddled as the basis for inherent male superiority, but physical strength alone does not translate to increased value in a Stone-Age setting. It is a useless attribute unless combined with the capacity of women to reproduce. Physical strength represents an obvious ability to transgress upon female rights, but it doesn't devalue the female contribution as such. Rather, physically overpowering women highlights the extraordinary value of women within and between tribes as a way of gaining genetic, social, or material advantage. It must also be considered that Stone-Age social systems where women were poorly treated (overworked, starved, beaten) is a disadvantageous trait that would likely compromise the ability of those women to reproduce and to raise productive new tribe members beyond a precarious infancy and into adulthood. Beyond the brutality of competing for women, we can assume the conditions in which they existed socially were favourable due to their inherent and equal value to the future of the tribe.

It has been theorised by Marxist scholars and anthropologists that disadvantage associated with female biological gender begins to emerge among tribes that adopted social systems of monogamous breeding pairs, based largely on sexual intercourse restrictions contingent on family relation. This system immediately limits the amount of women available for men to reproduce with, thus necessitating the capture or trade of unrelated women[7]. Brutal as this treatment may be, it seems likely that scarcity of childbearing-age women unrelated to men in the tribe elevated their inherent value. A further erosion of their individual autonomy, but still not a devaluation of their contribution. Their bodies and their ability to produce new tribe members were a hot commodity, and one in which men were considerably invested.

The tribes that implemented breeding restrictions gained advantages through hybrid vigour; the combining of vastly different genetic material that increases the likelihood of inherited beneficial traits, and gradually overpowered tribes with rudimentary, indiscriminate breeding systems.

It makes more sense that the devaluation of women, as well as the care and reproductive labour associated with them, emerges more decisively when humans began farming, stockpiling, trading commodities, and owning property[8]. American scientist and historian, Jared Diamond, repeatedly emphasises the dependence of social and gender inequality on contextual and environmental factors such as agrarian society rather than inherent deficiencies in any race or gender[9]. Diamond argues that having secure and readily available food supplies allows individuals to spend more time specialising in other tasks such as communicating, which results in language and commerce. Eventually, this specialisation connects some members of the community with education, knowledge, and power while others are left behind due to preoccupation with hard labour or childrearing. Thus, class and gender inequality emerge.

While there is a tendency to demonise the agricultural revolution for the resulting inequality that followed, I see it as a neutral development and one that should be expected considering the inventive nature and instinctive drive of humans to secure resources. The point is not to argue whether this was a mistake, but to demonstrate the earliest mechanisms by which care was devalued. Care and reproductive contributions were simply not scalable and not easily traded in the same way as agricultural commodities, so they didn't generate material wealth. They were also time intensive and prone to specialisation due to the physiological links women have to childbirth and care work such as breastfeeding. Women were not less capable of developing skills in literacy, trade, or governance, just far less likely to ever find themselves in a position to develop these skills. Nonetheless, the associations and stereotypes form that women are less intellectually capable or less well suited to these roles. The value of women and their work began to diminish relative to more typically male contributions that generated material wealth, resulted in ownership of property and, ultimately, access to power.

A new world order of trading goods and accumulating wealth made gendered labour division a clear disadvantage for women, both materially and in the sense of individual rights. While women specialised in reproductive and care labour, men specialised in generating commodities and found themselves in control of the resulting material wealth. Largely unencumbered by the care of babies and children, men were free to assume leadership positions and began playing a more prominent role in the course of human civilisation. Ancient civilisations were organised and economies built often through a uniquely male perspective.

Women remained tradeable objects beyond the Stone Age within legally-binding marriage systems that sanctioned the ownership of women and the free labour that came with them.

As populations increased rapidly, human life became expendable and cheaper in many cultures. With time, modern healthcare has come to mean human survival is much more assured than ever before. Childbearing-age women that had once secured the future of a tribe and signified its wealth and strength, what was a carefully protected and supported resource, became seen as an unproductive liability in modern economies and thus treated accordingly. Policy and supports for them were eroded and replaced by incentives to engage in labour that produced material wealth. The reproductive labour became simply a given – invisible and taken for granted.

Even as it became clear that reproductive labour was a huge disadvantage, women were essentially unable to limit their reproductive activity for centuries until birth control became commonplace. For most of human history, there has been no need to assign value to labour that was going to happen anyway. Only once women could control the number of children they had were they truly in a position to reduce their disadvantage. This is why women's empowerment sent birth rates in developed countries into freefall. Why do something that threatens your independence and financial security?

Even when women choose to have children, it is difficult for them to suddenly eschew incredibly successful evolutionary adaptations that developed over millions of years to ensure the survival of their offspring. Women who give birth find themselves at the mercy of ancient biochemical processes that drive them to feed the baby and undertake caregiving roles. We now know that postnatal biochemical and neurological processes work by making caring addictive for new mothers. Breastfeeding and contact with the baby elicits oxytocin, the same highly-addictive hormones that addicts chase[10].

A study following a cohort of 7,000 mother-infant dyads found that duration of breastfeeding was inversely related to instances of maternal neglect. Breastfeeding ensures routine releases of oxytocin that helps mothers form a positive association with their baby while also building a reward system that keeps them coming back for more. Vaginal birth is also known to result in a large oxytocin surge, which has been found to give mothers who experience a vaginal birth heightened receptivity to infant cues, at least in the short term. This is not to say that mothers who have caesarean sections or bottle feed are lesser mothers, but they do the same job with less hormonal encouragement. I see my own caesarean and difficult breastfeeding experience with my first born as a triumph in undergoing the transformation of becoming a mother with potentially less of a helping hand from hormonal processes.

Oxytocin makes caregiving feel good even though it may be hard. Broadly speaking, it ensures mothers act in self-sacrificial ways to ensure the survival of the infant. Where humans are ordinarily programmed to act in predominately self-serving ways, childbirth turns us into animals that serve others at our own expense. When neurobiological systems are in place to guarantee the care of children, the labour is going to happen anyway and there is less of an imperative to support it. Because of the biological nature of their contributions, women remain in a position of having little bargaining power.

In casting our minds back through human history we can begin to understand that the devaluation of women and care work arose not due to the nature of the sex but to a specific set of contextual conditions and, like a weed in optimal growing conditions, took over. If a particular set of social and economic conditions, occurring at least to some extent by chance, can subjugate half of the species then it is these economic and social conditions we must interrogate in our pursuit of 'equality'. Attempting to solve the issue simply by morphing women into men can only be described as an awfully basic and misogynistic approach.

The failure to assign value to reproductive and care labour, and to women themselves, means we now rely on women carrying out half of their work for free without even the safeguards of being 'provided for' or the social support systems that previously existed. Whole economies built by the endless and free production of human capital are now crumbling as birth rates plummet. Alternatively, the failure to legitimately value and support reproductive labour meant illegitimate and harmful forms of compensating this labour were allowed to emerge. Surrogacy and sex work almost always contain an exploitative dynamic whereby women who engage in this work have few options but to sell their bodily functions.

Through this slow march of human 'progress' the devaluation of women and their labour becomes a widely-held and entrenched belief accepted as a fact, rather than recognised for the baseless assumption it is. Based on the assumption that women and their work were inferior, the only liberation that was ever offered or envisaged for women was one where they could be less like themselves. Men and women alike came to believe that the only way to help women was to allow them to assimilate into a man's world. Leaders and everyday people today still struggle to identify this fatal flaw and recognise the reality of how badly this is now playing out for us.

Women first entered male-dominated professions often by impersonating men, such as Dr James Barry who was assigned female at birth in Ireland in 1795 but later transitioned to living as a man in order to gain acceptance to medical school. The irony is that this is still happening, in a sense, in 2025. Delaying children and reducing the amount of time we care for them is the modern-day impersonation of a man, carried out so that we may succeed in the modern economy and gain social status.

The question is not how do we change women and minimise womanhood and care work and their contribution but what mechanisms can we put in place that enable us to better value women and the entire spectrum of their contribution? What do women need to be able to comfortably perform their reproductive and care labour in whatever way they choose, and also engage in paid labour if they wish?

Erasing the inherent disadvantage of womanhood is a very different objective to simply minimising reproductive labour and motherhood. Pursuing the latter objective requires a set of 'solutions' that enable women to engage in less of their 'problematic' work and behaviours. These solutions then further embed women, our work, and our bodies as 'problematic' until this becomes a basic assumption. In turn, women have internalised this belief and become active participants in the diagnosis of ourselves as the problem. It causes us to take personal responsibility for systemic failings. We grow up believing we are the inherent problem. In some instances of firmly internalised misogyny, we have celebrated and encouraged our own erasure.

Solutions that assume women are fundamentally problematic, for example, in their tendency to assume caregiving roles, arise from the assumption that men and their work are the 'answer'. It's easy to see how everything about women is viewed as problematic in a context where men represent everything that is 'right'. For example, their ability to engage in full-time work, perform minimal caregiving, enter high-paying jobs and assume high-powered positions. If we are to develop solutions that truly value women, we must stop using men as a yardstick by which we judge women.

If our objective is to erase the inherent disadvantage of being a woman, to truly value women, we end up with a very different set of solutions on a very different trajectory. We would see policies that support women in both their paid and unpaid contributions. We would see high levels of public investment in supporting women financially while they are engaging in vital unpaid labour. We would see significant private investment in generating human capital that represents a vital input to any business or economy. We would see investment in the development of market-based mechanisms and policies that aim to financially support the unpaid care sector that underpins the economy. This isn't some utopian concept, these solutions are within our reach and many are already in practice around the world. Solutions that assure human reproduction will become absolutely unavoidable in the long run.

Women can and should have every opportunity but that includes the opportunity to be supported in motherhood. I'm writing this because I know our current approach to women's liberation is leaving many women behind. I know the stress and overwhelm that is making women sick. That women are being asked to do the impossible. I'm determined to change the trajectory of this approach for my daughters so they may experience support and pride when they are doing the most important job in the world.

The idea that caring for others isn't real work, that my value was only to be found in a paid workplace, has been the single greatest challenge of being a mother. It has undermined my daily efforts, seriously hampered my enjoyment of motherhood but also my growth as a person. With each question about when I was 'going back to work', with each line graph on the TV showing women's workforce participation lagging behind men, and with each news article about incentives to use childcare and its developmental benefits, I sank further and further into a place of confusion and despair. Was I doing this wrong? Was I missing something?

I thought delaying my return to paid work must have meant I was lazy, unambitious, and a bit backward. I've always gone against the grain, been less afraid to do my own thing but as my son grew older, I felt increasingly isolated. I couldn't understand how the work of actually caring for my kids and teaching them could feel so right but be so hard at the same time. After accumulating some on-the-ground experience of motherhood, I was shocked at how under-supported it was given its obvious importance. If this was supposed to be easy and effortless work that mothers could do on their own then I was much less capable than I thought. I wondered if maybe I just wasn't very good at it.

When my son turned one, I put him in daycare two days a week to return to paid work. I convinced myself that it was okay because basically every mother I knew had already returned to paid work. The Mother's Group had disintegrated and I needed to stop being lazy and 'get back to work'. Motherhood had started to feel like a dangerous space. We could use the money, I told myself. At this time, I was still driving an older model car I'd had since university, and we lived in a container home built by my husband. Costs were low but without a second income, we had fallen into a low-income category. We received a Healthcare Card and Centrelink payments but money was still tight. We weren't going hungry, but more money would make things easier, especially if we had another baby.

I was totally unprepared for the feeling of panic and loss that would creep up whenever I walked away from the daycare centre. I would spend the day feeling like I was missing a limb, and couldn't shake the look on my son's face when I would return to pick him up. If this was normal, and if most kids were in daycare, what was wrong with me?

In the end, it was the constant barrage of gastro and influenza, combined with welcoming a newborn baby into the home, that caused me to pull my son out of daycare. I still hadn't been able to put my finger on why I was uncomfortable with it, but the sickness was destroying our quality of life and I didn't want that to be my son's experience of toddlerhood or my daughter's experience of infancy.

After that, I was lucky enough to rely on grandparent care while I completed the odd freelance project. It wasn't much of an additional income but I loved writing and I thought it would look better on my CV than 'nothing at all', as I viewed it then. With two small children in tow, I had less time to dissect the philosophical issues and unanswered questions I'd had as a new mum. I became more settled in my identity and more at peace with the idea that I was doing things differently even though it was a lonelier road.

The issues and questions lay dormant until my husband required surgery for a neck injury he had sustained years earlier. He was in a huge amount of pain and the surgeon said he would be unable to continue working as an electrician. All of a sudden, money was fast running out and we had a decision to make – either I return to work full-time or we uproot the family so my husband could find different work.

We chose the latter and moved to southern New South Wales, about a 12-hour drive from family and friends, and three months before our third baby was born. The reality of raising children with little or no family support began to sink in soon after we arrived at the rural property where my husband was to work. Not long after we arrived, COVID lockdowns ensued.

By that stage, my eldest son was enrolled in four-year-old preschool but that year was significantly disrupted by COVID, and mostly I was home alone with all the kids. I tried to find nannies who would drive out to our farm for the day to help me with the kids but it was expensive. Also, I found it difficult to justify at the time given my work wasn't super lucrative. My kids had no connection to the series of nannies. The nannies didn't know my kids and weren't invested in them, how could they be?

Days on our own were beautiful in a sense but kind of sad at the same time. It was a revolving door of setting up activities, housework, meals, dealing with the emotions of little kids, dealing with my own emotions and doing it mostly alone. My husband was gone before we woke and often back after dark. I knew I wanted to be with my kids, but not like this. We weren't meant to be doing this alone.

Slowly but surely we settled into our community and made friends. The kids grew older and their needs slightly less intense. I found a nanny we adored and the kids formed a lovely bond with her. The day she came out was one we all looked forward to, and my youngest, Tully, has known Jess since he was born. It was so restorative just to be seen by another adult, have an extra pair of hands and someone else the kids gravitated to and with whom they had a warm connection. Her company kept me going and enabled me to continue doing odd jobs. We struggled to afford her and received no subsidy but by then, I viewed support for me as a non-negotiable cost.

My husband's new job meant we were more comfortable on a single income but we couldn't 'get ahead' in the same way dual-income families were. Our eldest son started school and my mum also moved to be closer to us. Mum continues to be an extraordinary help and puts in a huge amount of work. She is fit, strong, and the kids adore her. I'm extremely comfortable leaving them in her care. I'm not sure I would have coped without her help and I know many others don't have as much grandparent help as I do. Our friendships with families nearby strengthened over time and this meant I could connect with other mothers both outside the paid workforce and in paid work on a regular basis. I finally had the village I had desperately needed in the earlier years.

Still, the feelings of alienation from being largely outside the paid workforce continued in a broader cultural sense. I was being completely ignored in terms of family support and policy measures. I existed in a cultural blind spot. I was breastfeeding my kids to well over one year old and caring for children full-time before they started at a local preschool program consisting of one half-day for three year olds, and two school-length days for four year olds. I found myself unrelatable to others, but true to myself. I knew I was making people uncomfortable with their own decisions.

My identity and self-worth were no longer completely tied to my profession, and while I still enjoyed writing and felt compelled to do it, I didn't have the raging FOMO I'd had as a new mum. The world would still be there, my job would still be there, when my kids were older.

However, the conversations began to grate on me. "When will you go back to work? I wish I could just stay at home all day. It's such a luxury these days to be a stay-at-home mum. I'd go mad at home with the kids all day. They learn so much at daycare and do all sorts of activities I never do with the kids. They love daycare and they need to socialise."

I decided to get to the bottom of whether my kids should have been going to daycare to be developmentally normal and, contrary to public narratives, found the evidence base had not been able to establish benefits of daycare for children under three[11]. There was also evidence to suggest early and extensive daycare, especially where the quality and continuity of care could not be guaranteed, posed potential harm to babies' and toddlers' socioemotional development. The research was clear that preschool has undeniable benefits for children over three years old, particularly those who come from disadvantaged backgrounds and homes unable to deliver standard quality of care.

I was in disbelief. Why was there no transparent information or guidance around benefits and risks posed by formal care and education settings before school? Why were the needs of children and parents being so obviously dismissed by leaders? I finally realised that maybe the problem wasn't me all along.

By this stage, I'd been a mum long enough to know the work of caregiving is tough and relentless but the most rewarding work I have ever been involved in. I knew how wrong I had been about the work of care and how dismissive I had been. I could see how important my presence had been to our babies, toddlers, and children, and knew I had been grossly under-supported as a caregiver at times. I knew that going back to paid work would have been easier and more supported.

Then in 2021, I stopped at a set of traffic lights with two kids in the back seat, one in my belly, and one at school. Over the radio came a news story about a plan to deliver an extra year of primary school for four-year-old children. Both sides of government had signed on to the agreement which aimed to roll out full-time, free four-year-old preschool by 2030. It was hailed as a win for families who could work more and make more money, a win for kids developmentally and, most of all, a win for women who could and should get back to work ASAP. Something inside me snapped. I was white-knuckling the steering wheel and my heart rate lifted.

I was screaming on the inside because I was working. Raising my kids has been the greatest privilege but it has been the hardest work I have ever done. My body has been through so much, and I have been mentally pushed to the brink. I was screaming on the inside because I don't want to send my four year old to school a year early. It felt like a mistake. I wanted time with my kids.

I was screaming on the inside because I knew people were struggling financially, knew kids were starting school developmentally behind, and knew mental health was declining. I knew this was complicated, but we were looking for answers in all the wrong places. Increasing school years and hours, incentivising higher daycare attendance while minimising childhood and minimising motherhood was not the answer.

That night after the kids went to bed, I wrote a column for *The*

Australian that would launch me into a national debate about gender equality, family policy, and early childhood. It would be quoted in Parliament House and see me interviewed on national television and on countless podcasts. I would receive thousands of messages from women who felt the same and were grateful and relieved the issues were finally being called out. I would be verbally abused by women who felt personally attacked by the article. A high profile ABC presenter would publicly tell me to 'get fucked'. Another senior ABC reporter would privately message me with accusations that I was telling women they were 'fucking up their children'.

The article struck a chord in a big way – not because I was wrong but because I was right. It confirmed that it wasn't just me who felt this deep panic that this wasn't how motherhood was supposed to be. A new resolve settled upon me to not let this slide. To not let leaders, advocates, and members of the community continue to treat women as the problem.

It would be my life's work to fight for a parent's right to care for their children in the earliest years. No parent should be forced to outsource care work. No mother should be forced to return to paid work.

We could flip the entire script with three words: all mothers work.

CHAPTER THREE

Since the Apes Started Walking

A few million years ago, a colony of walking apes began doing things a little differently. Mothers started passing their babies to trusted family members to hold and even to feed. This was a significant divergence from other ape mothers who walked on all fours and aggressively refused to let anyone within arm's-reach of their baby. The walking apes knew they needed help when their babies became increasingly unable to grasp onto their thinning hair – a babe in arms meant no hands for foraging[12]. By enlisting the help of others, mothers became better fed and experienced less stress. They successfully raised babies through the longest and most high-dependency infancy in the animal kingdom. They started living longer and assisting others with birthing larger heads through smaller birth canals. The population of these walking apes persisted for millions of years and evolved to become what we know as hunter gatherers – they became human[13].

I relate strongly to my ancestral mother apes. After a few millennia, my needs are still essentially the same – a spare set of hands. Except here in the 21st century, the communities that once supported us are falling away and mothers are experiencing increased demands as well as less social support than ever before.

For almost all of human history, our lives have depended on this social support resulting in stubborn brain circuitry and neurochemical systems that still crave closeness and connection. Without connectedness and support for caregivers, without 'the village', we begin to experience mental and physical ill health on a global scale. Our brains are still in the Stone Age.

The profound and wide-ranging public health ramifications resulting from this lack of support for caregivers cannot be underestimated. Everybody alive today is a product of the care they received in their earliest years, and the quality of this care has lifelong impacts. We will almost certainly depend on others in times of ill health and old age. There is arguably no other public health issue that affects as many lives as caregiving.

The novel shared-care arrangement developed by the walking apes is one of our earliest examples of collaborative and pro-social behaviour that came to underpin human nature. This interdependency among humans continued for centuries in the form of tribes, villages, and then multigenerational households relying on a small labour force to run. Even in archaic societies with rudimentary technology, even as some of the most oppressive, impoverished, brutal, and patriarchal societies on Earth developed, social connectedness prevailed out of necessity and women remained in close proximity to intensive support networks.

That changed rapidly when the nuclear household began replacing most communal living arrangements or multigenerational households in developed Western nations by the 1950s. Industrialisation meant machines replaced much of the labour that had once required a team of people. Domestic and caring labour emerged from slavery as one of the worst paid and most undervalued jobs. As conditions improved for domestic workers, hired help became unaffordable for most households. The mother emerged as the sole housekeeper and primary carer of children. She became isolated in a role that had previously been shared among others for millions of years.

Mothers were beginning to deeply resent the impossible and lonely task assigned to them just as rubber really hit the road for career feminism in the 1970s[14]. Women ventured into the paid workplace to earn money, respect, and respite from their isolated caregiving roles. It was almost shameful to not take up the opportunity – caregiving, and motherhood with it, had become synonymous with oppression.

Governments around the world were eager to support a movement that actually made them money by creating a whole new labour force. Many countries boosted their Gross Domestic Product (GDP) by the creation of a whole new sector – the commodification of care meant that money changed hands for work previously conducted in the commons, that is under informal agreements with friends and family, or simply done for free by mothers[15]. Not only was the government in favour of the movement, but families saw the opportunity to earn more. Women saw a way to earn financial independence. It seemed like a win, win, win situation.

Women entering the workplace was a political and economic win, but it had a stratifying effect on the parent community. It reinforced and strengthened class divisions, starting with well-educated and wealthy mothers who were able to obtain paid work outside the home and could afford to pay someone else to look after their children and tend to domestic duties. A middle class of mothers emerged who either chose not to work outside the home or didn't earn enough to justify the costs of doing so. This middle class also included women who couldn't get a job outside the home due to limited experience or qualifications. The middle class would become known as 'stay-at-home-mothers' and would end up being stigmatised for their apparent failure to attain independence and respect offered by the women's liberation movement.

Lastly, the low-income mothers who were employed inside the home to look after the babies and children of other mothers who worked outside the home. These women were mostly people of colour, immigrant, or otherwise disadvantaged, often carrying out domestic work while also caring for their own children or relying on family members for informal care arrangements.

The catch-cry of breaking glass ceilings was far sexier than championing the rights of housewives and low-paid domestic workers[15]. The conservative movements that attempted to protect work inside the home as a right, a valuable function of community and crucial to broader wellbeing were often tarred by deeply-held prejudices and rigid beliefs that only women should perform care work. They became unpalatable to youth and the masses who were more easily won over with the oversimplified goal of freedom at any cost.

Consider the depiction of Phylis Schlafly by Cate Blanchett in the Netflix series *Mrs. America*. Phylis is racist, affluent, and believed in extremely traditional gender roles. There are several scenes that show her asking her husband for permission to attend public forums, condoning the abuse of women in marriage dynamics, undertaking very servitudinal acts such as removing her husband's jacket, giving him a foot rub, and having sex with him even when she doesn't want to. This is despite Schlafly accurately predicting many of the pitfalls of women's liberation, such as men and women becoming much more adversarial, the increasing instances of divorce, and the loss of support and the right to care for children.

On the other hand, actresses playing the leading characters of the liberal movement during the fight to pass the Equal Rights Amendment (ERA) are depicted as sexy and fun. It's easy to convey the negative sides of the conservative movement on screen, but it's much harder to show in a mini-series the long-term difficulty women now face in working two-shifts, struggling to get leave in the postpartum period, and struggling with identity.

There are some attempts to depict the conflict women faced – a marriage breakdown and the struggles of having a family in the context of motherhood being the source of oppression. There is a laugh-out-loud scene where members of the pro-ERA movement argue about whether or not housewives were the enemy. Apart from a line from Gloria Steinem—played by Rose Byrne—where she admits that "Revolutions are messy. People get left behind", the series falls short of adequately explaining the problem with the ERA.

The ERA sought to ensure all individuals were treated equally under the law, and you can see how on the surface this was appealing, but equity and equality are not the same thing. Equality means treating everyone the same, whereas equity acknowledges that people may have different starting points and needs, and therefore require tailored support to achieve equal outcomes. The ERA focused on equal treatment of women at the expense of equitable treatment. Through an equality lens women are expected to support themselves like a man while also undertaking largely unavoidable care and reproductive labour. An equitable approach to this same situation would see legal safeguards in place based on gender, which takes into account unique female experiences. For example, a legal entitlement to free postpartum physiotherapy or paid maternity leave would have been jeopardised under the ERA because this was an entitlement based on biological sex and one that would not be equally available to men.

The fundamental flaws of the equality movement in the 1970s were not well communicated and still poorly understood in contemporary, gender equality movements. The feminists are often characterised as noble and inspirational while the anti-feminists are considered petty, backward, and ridiculous.

While the feminist movement achieved great freedoms for privileged women by enabling them to enter jobs traditionally reserved for men, there were some serious undesirable side effects, particularly for women in paid and unpaid caregiving roles. Retaining a class of oppressed, low-paid women was a necessary precondition in the liberation of wealthy and educated, predominantly white women[16]. Middle-class women that eventually did enter the paid workforce were far less buffered from the pitfalls of the dual-income lifestyle that original career feminists had successfully carved out for themselves. They couldn't afford quality childcare arrangements and rather than hiring a cleaner, they set about working a double shift. One paid during business hours, and one unpaid after hours.

Rather than fighting to raise the status and value of 'women's work', which would have laid stronger foundations for an eventual liberation that captured all women regardless of race or class, early feminist movements simply enabled privileged women to access the advantages of 'men's work'.

Women's work wasn't just ignored in the process, it was deliberately downtrodden. Early feminists made clear attempts to disassociate themselves with it. In order to argue the case for women being able to work outside the home, the feminist movement often denigrated domestic duties and the act of caring for children in the home. Betty Friedman in *The Feminine Mystique* makes caring for children seem like a trivial and pointless half-life. 'Each suburban wife struggles with it alone. As she made the beds, shopped for groceries, matched slipcover material, ate peanut butter sandwiches with her children, chauffeured Cub Scouts and Brownies, lay beside her husband at night—she was afraid to ask even of herself the silent question—"Is this all?"'

Feminist philosopher, Simone de Beauvoir, likens the carer role to the torture of Sisyphus, a character of Greek mythology doomed by Zeus to repeatedly roll a boulder up a mountain and let it roll back down again. 'Few tasks are more like the torture of Sisyphus than housework, with its endless repetition,' De Beauvoir wrote in

The Second Sex. 'The clean becomes soiled, the soiled is made clean, over and over, day after day. The housewife wears herself out marking time: she makes nothing, simply perpetuates the present.'

Feminism is a modern example of a publicity campaign that irrevocably damaged the perception of caregiving. Yet for millions of years, caregiving in humans was valued as an equal and extremely valuable contribution to society.

In the context of relentless and disparaging attacks on care work, women start to internalise a sense of disrespect for caregiving and a belief that it is unimportant. They distance themselves from work or acts associated with femininity. Staff are employed for the 'lowly' work of childrearing.

Caregiving becomes increasingly difficult to distinguish from oppression and lower status. The status of caregiving has been so deeply damaged throughout history, that even as we raise the status of women and they become free of oppression, caregiving remains undervalued and exploited. In some ways, it is still oppressive, particularly when it is unpaid, but it is also a symbol of oppression and low status that makes people reluctant to align with it.

In the last few centuries, women have mostly clawed their way up the social or professional ladder by being more like men; distancing themselves from caregiving and adopting masculine values of individual success and wealth accumulation. Women may have been fully aware of certain injustices of their situation in early patriarchal societies but, for reasons discussed, were not in a position to challenge it. In the history of humans there has existed for many women a sense of accepting 'one's place in life'.

Around the time that literacy became widespread among women in the 15th century, it became clear women held a distinctly different view of the world. Still, it wasn't until the 19th century that the term 'patriarchy' was coined. It's an extremely short period in human history that we have even had a name for the social structures that influence our daily life and predetermine our futures.

By the time feminism was gaining momentum in the 1960s and 70s, women were acutely aware of the ways a patriarchal society was failing them. But even the feminist movement subscribed to the patriarchal definition of power and values; they sought empowerment by doing what men traditionally did. They placed themselves where power lay – in the workplace. Viewing power exclusively through the lens of the patriarchy makes perfect sense if there is no real awareness of the existence of an alternative worldview or the control this institution wielded over every aspect of women's lives, but feminists were well aware of this. Why did they perpetuate the dominance of the patriarchal lens? They didn't burn the patriarchy, they stepped right into it.

I contend it's because they knew they would have to beat men at their own game, or 'work the system' to reach positions of power from which they could then generate structural change. Women had to infiltrate the system in a sense, start writing policy, start hiring other women, start working as doctors and lawyers and politicians and journalists. They did this successfully and in large numbers. The argument that had been wielded for centuries, that women simply didn't belong in places of power, weren't smart enough or physically couldn't do the work, was rendered null and void.

As a result of women's workforce participation, many women in developed and Western areas of the world now experience fewer injustices in policy decisions, healthcare, and opportunity. The world view shifted to encompass a much better balance of masculine and feminine influence and perspectives. But the work is far from over, with men and women in positions of power and throughout the community still failing to assign value to caregiving in a meaningful way. It is still grossly overlooked and viewed as a weakness, something to be outsourced and minimised as much as possible.

Rather than valuing and legitimising the care work women do, whole institutions have been built in the last 60 years to enable women to further distance themselves from their caregiving roles in favour of paid work. The pendulum has swung so far that a novel form of oppressing women has emerged with mothers forced to undertake paid work for financial security, in some countries just weeks after giving birth, even when they may have desperately wished to care for their new babies and growing families. The avoidance and contempt of caregiving has made men even slower to share the unpaid work than they might have been if it was recognised appropriately in social policies and workplaces.

Sadly, we still see the solution to gender equality as solely based on 'fixing women' by reducing their caregiving responsibilities and increasing their paid work participation, putting them in the 'right kind of jobs', rather than 'fixing men' or engineering the system to more equally redistribute unpaid work or better remunerate unpaid work. It's as if the feminist movement called halftime and then forgot to get back on the field and play the rest of the game. The fight to give all women more choice, to make life better for all women, has only just begun.

I contend that when women entered the workplace, they had to internalise a devaluation of caregiving. They actually had to embody the belief that caregiving wasn't important in order to endure and overcome the inner turmoil caused by their conflicting roles. A deep division emerged between women in paid work and women in unpaid work. It's possible that women in positions of power and leadership began to see caregiving as a lack of ambition and a contribution not worthy of support. They focused on helping women whose decisions aligned with their own resolutions in prioritising paid work.

As policies and the demands of growth economies tipped in favour of women entering paid work and incentivised this, the social fabric that might have supported women outside paid work began to wear thin. People were at home less and therefore had scant time for leisure, community, food preparation, and volunteering. The neighbours and family and friends who might have been in unpaid caregiving roles, working alongside each other during the day, disappeared to the office. Mothers who remained in unpaid caregiving roles became increasingly isolated and unsupported. As a result, experiences of mental illness like postpartum depression begin to increase but it would not be included in the American Psychiatric Association's *Diagnostic and Statistical Manual of Mental Disorders* until 1994.

Awareness and recognition of postpartum mental health struggles wouldn't become widespread until around the turn of the millennium. Data shows postpartum depression continues to increase at an alarming rate[17]. Many mothers returned to work out of desperation to connect with others in an increasingly fragmented community.

When women entered paid work it created this assumption that what they were doing before wasn't work and wasn't necessary. It introduced a dangerous and misleading binary that care and reproductive labour was 'not working'. This is partly based on this underlying capitalistic assumption that if it's unpaid it's not really work. It's also based on the language that emerged. Phrases such as, 'I've got to go to work', 'I'm going back to work' or 'I'm having some time off'.

Even today, focusing on increasing female workforce participation is still considered a progressive standpoint despite obvious flaws in this approach continuing to affect our daily lives. It's a popular party line and now framed as a policy for 'the people', for 'working families' and 'struggling families', when in reality it is an extractive policy that gives families no other choice but to work more and more. It's also becoming apparent that there are limitations as to how far this approach can take us in terms of gender equality.

We've developed a kind of tunnel vision where we don't know how else to achieve gender equality so we refuse to acknowledge the drawbacks of a society that is increasingly reliant on dual incomes and increasingly outsourcing childcare to the market from younger ages. This tunnel vision has sucked funding and research away from a wide range of alternative, supplementary measures that could prioritise the wellbeing of women, children, and families.

Ultimately, our evolutionary need for connection still exists and remains necessary for healthy brain development even though we no longer face the obvious physical dangers that shaped our brains. Survival may no longer be intrinsically linked to physical closeness and emotional connection between caregivers and babies, but our psychological wellness remains reliant on these conditions. Babies and mothers don't suddenly evolve in the space of 50 years to adapt to completely novel childrearing and mothering practices.

Our brains expect the same support, nurturing, and close contact with our children as our ancestors would have experienced. With the right policy, market-based mechanisms and individual awareness, our needs can be supported, public health outcomes improved and our overall productivity lifted. Caregiving and motherhood need not be oppressive, harmful, and disrespected roles, but rather a vital tool in building a healthier society.

CHAPTER FOUR

Care is Real Work

From the toilet, I hear my three-year-old daughter yell, "Mum, Tully's got a knife!" The kids had been stirring cupcake batter when I left to use the loo, leaving the door of the dishwasher I had been unpacking, slightly ajar. As I thunder back down the hallway toward the kitchen, I realise that my one-year-old son, Tully, must have plucked the sharpest knife from the open dishwasher[18].

I find him laughing and waving the knife precariously close to his eyeballs. I get low and begin my approach like I'm trying to subdue a psychotic gunman. Stealthy and swift, but not fast enough to startle him. Soothing him with my words. I get the knife, nobody is hurt, but it's only 9:30am.

There will be several more close shaves before the day is through, and a few misses. I will clean, teach, hold, cook, yell, laugh, and yawn my way through the day. I think the biggest lie of my life is that all of this isn't real work. The word 'work' doesn't do it justice, even seems to cheapen the experience of raising a human life, but in a rudimentary sense it is very much a form of labour. A life-altering, exhausting, rewarding, unseen and often lonely labour.

It's a constant battle with multiple sets of emotions – our own and those we care for. Personally, I have found the work of caregiving to be more emotionally than physically exhausting. I know I have chosen to be there for most of it – the most idyllic and the messiest of moments. Not everybody can afford this time, professionally or financially, and that's a problem we return to repeatedly in this book. Not everybody will choose this time, but it should be a choice, nonetheless. To what degree each of us actually engages in care work does not change the fact that it is both valuable and difficult. That it is the most challenging, meaningful, and labour-intensive work we will ever do.

To understand how care work, in all its complexity, came to be so badly dismissed and degraded, I only have to cast my mind back to myself 20 years ago, where I had absolutely no clue about the physical and mental demands of caregiving. I only saw mothers in public and paid no attention to the effort it took for them to get out the door. There was no way of seeing the hours they spent behind closed doors teaching, instructing, cooking, cleaning, organising and caring for others. Motherhood and care work is really something you have to experience first-hand to understand its difficulty and its importance. It's hard to recognise the value of care if you have never cared for someone.

As many children do, I took my own mother for granted. As the youngest of her two daughters, I never saw her caring for a baby or young child. The first baby I saw latch onto a nipple was my own. I had never changed a nappy before, and didn't identify much with the term 'stay-at-home mum' because I was raised on narratives that frame mothers working in the home as kind of unnecessary, fluffing about, neurotic, sad alcoholics. 'Housewife' had become a derogatory term in my time. I was raised to have a career and we skimmed over the details of 'just being a mother'.

My internalised beliefs that caregiving wasn't a valuable or worthy use of time continued to solidify into adulthood. I had enjoyed far more opportunity than women who had gone before me. I had an excellent education, sporting opportunities, and my pick of any career that took my fancy. At times, I would joke about becoming a 'housewife' or a 'stay-at-home mum' when I had wanted to give up on my exams at school and university.

I was 24 years old when I began to think more about babies. It was an unexpected development given just five years earlier I had been drinking punch out of a garbage bin at university. Babies had been the furthest thing from my mind after I graduated, crammed my belongings into a tiny hatchback and drove across Queensland to my first posting as a reporter in Mount Isa.

I know it's often said women are 'socially conditioned' to want to care for others and have babies, but I think any woman born in the last 40 years has experienced almost the opposite – a very career- or work-centric conditioning. To achieve equality by being the closest possible thing to a man. If anything, I was socially conditioned to work a 40-plus hour week. Nobody in my social circle had kids. There seemed to have been very few reasons for a woman of my age and stage in career to really feel like throwing a baby into the mix.

And yet, there it was, this animal feeling of wanting my own kids. I would later recognise this feeling when I would later wish for the positive tests of planned pregnancies with every fibre of my being. There is a level of social expectation that women will have babies and assume the task of caring for them, but we must recognise that social conditioning is in a constant, complex interplay with biology. We certainly don't ovulate and lactate based on social conditioning, and these processes are primary driving forces when mothers assume caregiving roles. When we respond to hormones, we aren't 'oppressing ourselves'. Anyone who has heard their own baby in distress knows this is a clear case of stress and adrenaline hormones flooding our body rather than a social expectation.

So, I worked hard and took risks, but in the midst of building a career, and despite my disparaging views of caregiving roles, I also knew I wanted children. The 'want' persisted until it became a 'need' and I could no longer imagine my life without them. I assumed I would be a 'working mum' donning a blazer and breezing out the door of a morning. Even created a vision of motherhood in which my current life didn't change much and the children didn't seem to feature heavily. Bizarrely, I didn't account for the huge amount of time that goes into raising children. Didn't realise how much they would need me. How much I would want to be with them, and how much I would dislike leaving them.

These visions of a breezy motherhood were shattered when the doctor pulled my firstborn out of a six-inch incision in my abdomen. I walked into the delivery ward as a career woman but once inside, I became someone who frenetically milked her own colostrum. I was blindsided by an incredibly successful evolutionary adaptation – hormones that would incessantly drive me to keep the baby alive at all costs. Neurobiological systems that would scream at me to find the baby, even though my head knew he was in the Neonatal Intensive Care Unit (NICU) two floors below me, requiring machines to help him breathe, and that I was receiving magnesium sulphate intravenously in Intensive Care to prevent my body convulsing. Still, my whole body searched for the baby. I compulsively checked a photo of him my husband sent to my phone.

Children were always an obvious fatal flaw in dominant feminist theory – career feminism[19]. The way a baby craves its mother's milk is quite an inconvenience if one is trying to work like a man. The way a baby's cry can set off a mother's adrenal glands, triggers her letdown reflex like a fire hydrant, becomes something to be studiously ignored. Millions of years of evolution, the intricate neurobiological adaptations that shape a sophisticated and lasting bond between a birth mother and her newborn. All but an afterthought in an otherwise compelling ideology that has transformed the lives of women around the world. The way a woman's body searches for the baby she birthed just doesn't fit the career-feminist agenda.

It has taken me nine sleep-deprived years to put my finger on the cultural blind spots, social attitudes and policy failings that robbed me of many motherhood joys. Contrary to popular feminist theory, politicians, and gender-equality advocates we hear every day in the news, it's actually not the care work itself that ails us but rather the conditions in which the care work is carried out. Sure, motherhood is tough and all, but we can do hard things with the right support. At the root of every dismissive attitude and policy failure is the devaluation of care. Feeling undervalued, unsupported, and invisible in our role as mothers is the root cause of our angst and distress.

We are undergoing a steady process of eliminating the motherhood penalty by minimising motherhood itself, rather than reducing the penalty. This was a deliberate strategy of the earliest career feminists, and it is understandable. It was necessary to deny their own biology and minimise the needs of infants and postpartum mothers in order to be accepted into the existing power structure – the paid workplace.

I was in a similar mode of denial throughout my first pregnancy, saying things like "the baby is coming to live with us so it will need to fit in with our lives". I prided myself in the way my pregnant belly barely showed and how I still went to the gym and how my life had not altered during pregnancy. I hid my pregnancy at work and then eventually when I did tell my boss, I asked for six months' unpaid leave.

It really is extraordinary, the mental gymnastics I performed during this time to reassure myself that nothing much would change and everything was within my control. I was a product of a society where pregnancy and motherhood had become far less visible. Where motherhood was presented as something to be restrained and hidden away.

My first indication that my theories were about to crumble came at 37-weeks pregnant. At a routine weekly check-up it was discovered that my blood pressure was out of control. My body was having an abnormal immune response to the placenta, a condition known as preeclampsia. It soon became apparent that no amount of drugs were going to be able to bring my blood pressure into a safe range. I was booked in for an induction of labour the following day but that night, blood tests indicated that my organs were failing. I remember thinking: *Wow, this has really gotten out of hand.* It's a thought that, on reflection, pretty much sums up my early years as a new mother.

Oscar was born in the early hours of the morning. Not only was I completely and irrevocably changed by the arrival of my son, I was obsessed with him. I had no control over my desire to be with him and to keep him alive. As soon as we were well enough, we were reunited for the first feed.

Relief flooded through me to feel the weight of his body on mine. I was desperate to feed him but it quickly became apparent I had no idea how. It was all so clumsy and required several sets of hands reaching in to sandwich my nipple into his tiny mouth.

Our breastfeeding relationship was fraught with struggle – mastitis, tongue-tie surgery, and weigh-ins for the entire 10 months I persisted. Everything seemed a challenge, but mostly the feeding. I had truly believed that in motherhood, like much of my life so far, if I brought my A-game to it I'd at least be able to manage, if not crush it. It was such a blow to my self-esteem to realise just how unmanageable things were. I had totally underestimated the act of caring, a baby's constant need for care, the absolute stamina a carer must have. How much help I would need.

I remember clearly how shocked I was at how soon after a feed he would need to be fed again. With raw nipples, I would cringe if he stirred or when someone wheeled him back into the room. I could never get a sense of accomplishment, could never tick that job off for the day, because the job was never done. We were drowning from the beginning. The individual achievements of my life, the goal-setting and ticking-off tasks were of no use in the foreign, new land of motherhood.

We went home at about five days postpartum at my insistence and having demonstrated to the nurses that I could inject myself with the anti-blood-clotting medication. A few days later, I presented back at the hospital with a raging case of mastitis brought on by pumping too much milk with the breast pump. Four weeks later, we would return to hospital again after Oscar contracted Viral Meningitis (Parechovirus), a condition that can quickly kill a newborn. Oscar survived the illness, but I was already cooking up a new one – postnatal anxiety and depression.

Motherhood is a challenging and life-altering experience at the best of times; throw in a few curve balls and disaster can ensue. Add to that the assumption most of us carry that this work is easy and effortless. Add to *that,* the isolation of mothers in a role that has been shared among others and intensively supported for millions of years, and we begin to realise how much we stack the odds against parents.

As a new mother who remained in a caregiving role long after my peers returned to paid work, I remember the distinct feeling of having been lied to. Having realised that I could not have it all. I found myself isolated from the community and conflicted by engaging in work I had been conditioned to consider of little real value. It was a struggle to find fulfillment in work that I had been taught was oppressive or 'beneath me'. I was unable to access my well-established reward systems based on work performance, completion of tasks, individual achievements, and external validation. The promotions and the key performance indicators and the awards were no use to me now. Feminism, as I knew it, had only served me as long as I acted like a man.

I eventually clawed my way back to the one thing that made sense—paid work—only to find that giving my son to strangers to look after was something I could never get used to. The tightening in my chest and throat. The sadness in his eyes when I left. The look of desperation when I returned. The senselessness of bringing a child into the world only to pay someone else to care for him.

It was increasingly evident to me that raising my kids was the most important work of all—shaping the next generation, the guidance of our collective future, the nurture of precious lives, the cultivation of our most important global resource—yet it didn't seem to be supported. My contribution was invisible and ignored. Why don't we value care? More worryingly, why had I not valued care for so long?

Then incentives to use childcare and pressure to return to the paid workplace became an extension of the idea that care work was not as important as our paid work. While institutional childcare is now a financial imperative for many, it is fundamentally based on the assumption that care work is to be subjugated in favour of other work. It's the modern-day equivalent of wet nursing.

The idea that the care of a baby or young child can be easily outsourced and carried out in bulk is also fundamentally rooted in the belief that the work is easy and somewhat meaningless. The idea that a person previously unknown to my child—and almost certainly transient in their life—could look after them together with many other children without consequence and perhaps even with benefit, seemed to further cheapen my role as a parent and caregiver. As if I were optional, that they could do without my presence for extended periods during the day.

The trend towards outsourcing childcare has supported women in their paid work contribution but left them grossly under-supported in their unpaid contribution. As much as formal childcare is now part of the overall support ecosystem for parents, we cannot lose sight of the fact that in some ways it also undermines the concept and the value of parenting.

Childcare policy is rooted in the idea that parents could and should be doing something more valuable with their time. With each new childcare incentive, it feels like a slow process of making parent-carers redundant. The agenda is clear – you're of more value in the paid labour force.

Despite constant messaging that I was of more value in the paid workplace, the older my kids got and the deeper into motherhood I went, my conviction that caregiving was important only grew stronger. I am a fixture in their day. They might not always need me, but they know I'm there. An omnipresence. A constant.

There is just something about 'being there'. It's a sleepy toddler crawling into my lap after lunch. A three year old making up a song where I am the audience. Me putting sunglasses on the dogs and making the kids laugh. Striking a match to show them how bright the flame burns.

Nobody wants to talk about the value of that. We can't talk about the benefits of unpaid care work as a societal contribution or acknowledge it without parents in paid work feeling judged or triggered. I can't talk about the value of the small moments without that being trivialised as a luxury. I can't talk about this without being accused of romanticising oppression or undermining the fight for equality. The more the benefits of care work are censored or denied, to protect policies and the feelings of parents in paid work, the more we start to collectively believe the value isn't there.

The more we fail to acknowledge the benefit of parental time with very young children, or even deny it, the trickier it is to justify public policy that supports this. If consistent and fairly constant access to parents becomes considered quite unnecessary for babies and children, how do we argue for policies like extended paid and unpaid parental leave? Why would a government implement this policy if there is no benefit?

In this environment, parents internalise the message that care work is less valuable because it is largely unsupported in public policy. It is well established that parenting values and practices have a tendency to shift in line with policy – making childcare cheap or free has been associated with parents changing behaviours and placing lower value on parental care[20]. The way our values change in response to government policy is a well-documented phenomenon observed around the world.

When governments use policy to influence the decision-making of individuals without necessarily mandating certain behaviours, it's called 'nudge policy'. Freedom of choice is at least superficially maintained but people are steered towards certain behaviours. Family policy has been shaped specifically to increase the hours we outsource the care of our babies and young children, nudging parents—mainly women—to increase paid work hours.

Childcare subsidies were the single biggest budget commitment of the Federal Labor Government in the 2023/2024 budget[21]. That's a nudge. The Commonwealth Paid Parental Leave Scheme has a work test that effectively requires women to return to paid work between having babies in order to be eligible for payments. That's a nudge. The Paid Parental Leave Scheme only provides leave payments for 22 weeks, set to increase to 26 weeks by 2026-2027. That's a nudge. The 2023 Federal Senate Work and Care Inquiry clearly favoured policies and made recommendations that support dual-income families rather than families where one parent contributes unpaid care and labour. That's a nudge.

Members of government continue to perpetuate the misconception that formal childcare is clearly beneficial for children under three years of age. That's a nudge.

What starts out as one nudge turns into a series of little nudges that end up as a great big push.

This kind of nudge policy may eventually equalise paid workforce participation between men and women, but at what cost? Is this genuine equality that truly values paid and unpaid contributions? What message does this policy direction send to parents and carers?

The ethics of nudge policy are highly debatable, particularly when it nudges families in the direction of child-rearing practices that have well-documented negative health outcomes for both parents and children. Especially when that nudge policy is underpinned by an understaffed, low paid, and disrespected industry.

Rather than using nudge policy to nudge more men into unpaid work, and more equally redistribute unpaid care work between men and women, or nudge policy to remunerate unpaid care work, it has been used to increase workforce participation and to increase the commercialisation of care of our youngest and most vulnerable.

Failure to acknowledge the value of this intimate, day-to-day care in public policy is also reflected in workplace cultures that see caregiving as a liability. If care work is not legitimised by public policy, if there are not enough legislated work protections for those who do it, there is no standard set about how to value and support employees who carry out unpaid care work.

Now that we have most families being forced to or choosing to carry out paid work while outsourcing unpaid care work, more and more narratives circulate that support this situation. This means that often when families commit to contributing unpaid care and labour themselves instead of outsourcing, they are dismissed. Even if they must make difficult financial decisions such as delaying the purchase of a home, moving closer to support or cheaper housing, even moving for a pay rise for the sole earner, they are characterised as privileged and as living in luxury. Some families save for years to fund time to raise their children before planning a pregnancy. Dismissing people in unpaid care work as 'privileged' can ignore the fact that many are living off minimal means to afford this time with their children. It can be demoralising for those investing their life savings in their child's earliest years to hear their choices being dismissed in this way.

Almost all of the value I am now able to see in caregiving has come from lived experience, a concerted effort to turn away from cultural expectation and instinct. Messaging from the outside has only served to confuse the situation and make me doubt myself. As the months turned into years, it became easier to see the value in what I have been doing, but it took time and hindsight. The early years of motherhood were difficult because deep down I didn't even value what I was doing. I had internalised a devaluation of care. I often felt like I was failing because I expected it to be easy. Care work is an absolute skill that takes years to develop. Once I assigned my role its true value and degree of difficulty, the feelings of failure melted away.

Kids are such a long, long game. There are little bright spots all along the way, but sometimes it can be hard to see the results in such incremental work. It's easier to not assign value to something that is very difficult to measure or when progress is hard to identify. The skills and knowledge and maturity can bubble and grow beneath the surface, so that you're not always sure they are there until inevitably it surfaces. The skills can be painfully slow.

Then, gradually, enough time passes that you get a sense of how fleeting their dependencies are and it knocks the wind right out of your chest. To see their soul start shining through and their tiny chests puffing out bravely in a world that can be so dark. To see them grapple with their uncertainty and their inevitable humanness. To get to know the spirit that you have imbibed with your own light and dark. Those are the rewards you cannot imagine at the newborn nappy changes. Most of the time, while parenting, it's impossible to know what you are working towards. It's not some tangible and obvious reward like a paycheque on Thursdays. It's not instant gratification.

Care work has real economic value and quantifiable health benefits. It creates efficiencies that translate to monetary gain, and all of this we will discuss in future chapters. But there are elements of care that are so personal and private, so impossible to trace to any precise moment, that they will forever be immeasurable. A funny moment shared or an encouraging nod. A surge in oxytocin when they come in for a hug or show you their artwork. Watching them succeed after they have struggled to complete a task. The smallest moments, almost imperceptible gestures, accumulate and eventually add up to define our existence. Our interactions with those that care for us, and those we care for, alter our life trajectory.

When we consider the real magnitude of care work and its profound implications, we begin to realise that the 'sad housewife' narrative is misplaced. 'Housewives' were not frustrated with the work of caring *per se,* but rather the disconnection from community, support, respect, personal autonomy, and financial independence their work entailed. Caring for our kids is some of the most meaningful work we will ever do. By certain definitions, cultivating a sense of self in another is the meaning of life. Passing on your experience of the world, the giving of your life and time. You don't have to be a parent to do that, but most often this is how it occurs.

When parents carry out care work in a context where it is dismissed and minimised, it's easy to lose sight of the importance and meaning. Parents can become starved of community and validation. It's only a matter of time before we are forced to seek belonging outside of our caregiving role – most commonly, in our careers and workplaces. Humans are social beings at the end of the day; a certain amount of external validation sustains us. We thrive on seeing ourselves through the eyes of others and being reassured that our place in the community is secure.

I think this is what most women mean when they say they went back to paid work to "save their sanity". They sought connection. They wanted to feel valued. They wanted to return to the kind of work from which they derived their sense of self-worth. And if we're going to emphasise the element of choice early feminists fought so hard for – is returning to work to save your sanity and sense of self really coming from a place of choice? No. It's a decision made under duress. The kids and the work aren't the problem, it's the *context*. The lack of support for a role that is deeply underestimated. Only when we correctly diagnose this problem can we remedy it and create genuine choice.

In the previous chapter we looked at the devaluation of care on a macro level – the historical, cultural, and economic forces at play. Now, in this chapter we have taken the devaluation of care to a micro or individual level. It took me years to unlearn the damaging attitudes I held towards care and parenting. I have been through such a revelation yet still catch myself denigrating the care work I do on a daily basis and underestimating the value of what I have achieved. In darker moments, I think I will never truly be able to value the care work I do and might never feel fully feel at ease in the moment.

If we are to improve conditions for parents and caregivers more broadly, it requires each and every one of us to identify exactly how our social conditioning around care work is playing out for us. Only then can we take solutions and attitudes into the community. As with so many things, change can start with us.

CHAPTER FIVE

Valuing Care Work

If our failure to properly value care work is at the root of gender inequality and declining human health, then finding ways to value care becomes critical. When we understand how and why we devalue care in both a societal sense and individual level, it's easier to change.

Everyday language

The best place to start when it comes to valuing care is to notice the everyday language we use in relation to care work. Have you ever described your parental leave as 'taking time off', as if it's some form of holiday? Have you struggled to describe yourself as 'just a mother' while on maternity leave, embarrassed that people might think this is all you do? Have you noticed the images that 'staying home with the kids' conjures – watching TV, lounging about, messy buns, dishes?

It might not be our own language but that used by people in positions of power and influence. A key example of this can be seen in the Women's Economic Equality Taskforce's (WEET) 10-year plan to 'unleash the full capacity and contribution of women to the Australian economy'[22]. The 2023 report repeatedly frames unpaid carers as an opportunity-cost in the order of $128 billion and as not fully contributing[23]. The Taskforce recommendations will apparently help to 'unlock the value of women's full economic participation'. There were some positive policy recommendations in the report, such as extending paid parental leave; however, recommendation points such as this were weakened and undermined by the language used to deliver it. Why extend parental leave if unpaid carers are such a drain on the economy?

We must start valuing care work by absolutely refraining from characterising unpaid caregivers as an idle part of the population who require 'unleashing' or 'unlocking'. This language is underpinned by either a lack of understanding of what care work actually entails or a failure to place value in it. The taskforce cannot *unleash* caregivers because they are already engaged in the full-time work of caring for children. Caregivers are not an untapped resource reclining on a lounge. Entering paid work is simply a process of parents exchanging one form of legitimate work for another.

WEET's case was clear to me when I finished reading the report. I can't see how any unpaid caregiver reading that report could deduce anything other than 'I'm holding Australia back by remaining in unpaid labour'. All the way through the report, I caught myself thinking, *I'm bad for the economy, I'm a chronic under-performer and I'm wasting my high-quality tertiary education. The plan is for women like me to get back to work, preferably full-time.*

We must call out language that suggests people in caregiving roles aren't contributing, aren't pulling their weight economically. These continue to be the most harmful attitudes towards women being perpetuated today. This degrading characterisation of our work through language is a huge part of the reason we can't attract necessary political support and funding for the work of care. This underpins the poor-quality childcare and aged care thousands of Australians use every day. This language makes men less inclined to engage in caregiving roles. If women need 'unleashing' from care responsibilities, do men need 'leashing' into caregiving? When we are trying to redistribute unpaid labour more equally, this terminology is making care work sound more unpalatable than ever. To describe those performing arguably the most critical task of humankind—nurturing the next generation and caring for our most vulnerable with grace and compassion—as just waiting to be unleashed, is the ultimate insult.

The language in this report was all the more dangerous because it didn't come from a man with little lived experience of caregiving or some misogynist who might be expected to devalue a woman's contribution; these words came from highly esteemed and respected women like Sam Mostyn, who have positioned themselves as advocates for women and care feminists. In 2021, Mostyn gave a Press Club Address which, at first glimpse, seemed to signify a shift from career to care feminism in the highest echelons of Australian power. "In Australia, we like to tell ourselves that we are the Lucky Country … and yet among our vast natural resources, possibly the most underrated, undervalued has been the unpaid [and low-paid] work of women," she said. "We are 'lucky' to have benefited from that for so long."

Sadly, by the end of her address, I realised the only way Mostyn was proposing to better support unpaid caregivers was by getting them out of unpaid work. She framed their care contribution as a problem that could and should be minimised rather than a critical societal function. Astonishingly, she pointed to 'freeing up' people with care responsibilities as a way of increasing community wellbeing. Mostyn's speech was described as a 'brave new vanguard of care feminism', but at its core this is career feminism in a 'care' cloak. Mostyn's guiding principle is still about subjugating unpaid care work in favour of paid work, rather than implementing policy that acknowledges the unpaid contribution is valuable and irreplaceable. When this basic assumption pops up at every turn, it's contagious. We are more likely to repeat and believe phrases we commonly hear.

The examples of this language in the public sphere are endless. Former Victorian Premier Daniel Andrews spoke about "unlocking the potential of women". Independent MP Zoe Daniels said, "Women want to work. We simply must enable them". Liberal MP Hollie Hughes said, "Not all of us want to sit at home with our three-month-old watching *Bluey*." Interim CEO of The Parenthood, Jessica Rudd, said women's skills "are left to atrophy on a playmat full of Duplo".

Phrases such as these fail to recognise that women who are not in paid work are still engaging in a legitimate form of labour. Mothers who are not in paid work are often already completely utilised fulfilling critical unpaid labour roles. There is no larger industry or economic contribution than unpaid care work, worth approximately $650.1 billion dollars to the Australian economy. Instead of recognising this enormous contribution, the language we are immersed in frames people contributing care work as part of the 'problem' politicians and leaders are trying to solve.

The more we are exposed to this language, the more care work becomes a regressive kind of liability in our own mind, even though we are constantly reminded in our day-to-day care experience that we are indispensable in our role of looking after others. We end up feeling that we need to avoid care work or at least hide the unpaid work we do to avoid being identified as 'the problem'. In wanting to not be associated with the labour, we then find ourselves in a position where we cannot ask for support with our unpaid contributions.

Because women have been working hard to establish and prove themselves in the paid workforce, and in doing so attempting to hide care and reproductive labour, our unpaid labour became even easier to exploit than when housewives were seen as engaging in a legitimate role. It's very difficult to demand rights to engage in something if we are busy denying its importance or pretending it's not affecting our ability to perform paid work. Derogatory language has created a situation where women have convinced themselves they need to work twice as hard because half the work they do is 'worthless'. In reality, women are giving the economy more for less.

Difficult as it may be, the solution here is to stop using language that describes care work as 'doing nothing' or a 'luxury'. Changing the words we use to describe care and the people who do it is absolutely critical to better valuing the work. Parenting and caring for children is not 'time off'. It is critical that we begin to describe our paid jobs as our 'paid work' because this better reflects that we make other contributions which are unpaid, as opposed to the binary of 'working' or 'not working'.

As a mother, when I am asked what I 'do', I am practising saying, "I care for our children" rather than "I'm just at home with the kids at the moment". We don't have to justify the role of caregiver as being 'temporary' and reassure others that we will be back to 'real work' very soon. It's also not 'just' looking after children; it's a huge, important job that should never be prefaced by the word 'just'.

'Stay-at-home mum' versus 'working mum'

It's also time to phase out the terms 'stay-at-home mum' and 'working mum'. As far as I understand, very few mums actually appreciate or identify with these terms. Mums in paid work don't like being called 'working mums' because it highlights a double standard when we don't call dads in paid work 'working dads'. The term 'working mum' perpetuates the idea of a special subset of mothers and prevents us from ever completely normalising mums in paid work. If we recognise that all mothers work, there is no need to describe a mum as 'working'.

It's also a term that inadvertently further invisibilises care work because mums in paid work are also working before and after they actually arrive at their paid job. If a mum is working basically at all times then there is no need to call her a 'working mum' because it's a given.

And as a mum who's been caring for my kids for the last nine years, I think the term 'stay-at-home mum' poorly reflects my actual role. I do not 'stay-at-home' and unpaid caregiving and labour is a whole lot of important work. We can say we're 'staying at home' when we're sick or we don't want to go to the party, when we are hanging back, but not when we're performing a vital societal function. I'm out and about, I volunteer, I'm contributing. 'Stay-at-home' sounds like I'm not participating or I'm permanently sick.

This harmful language binary of the stay-at-home mum (a 'SAHM', as it is commonly known on social media) and the working mum also has a clear implication that you're either working in paid work, or you're not working and 'staying at home'. This makes the labour of unpaid caregiving less visible and less valuable. They are diametrically opposing terms that do mums in both paid and unpaid work a disservice the world over, because all mums still do the bulk of unpaid work and are inherently still disadvantaged by that. Making the unpaid care contribution invisible or 'lesser' means the policy response is inadequate to support mothers in whatever capacity they work.

Yet the terms persist, even though they are sexist, unhelpful, and inaccurate. The term SAHM is fast becoming derogatory, similar to the use of the word 'housewife'. We inadvertently minimise and devalue the caregiving role by saying things like, "I went back to work because I needed mental stimulation and it was so boring", as if the only people who would remain in a caregiving role are unambitious and simple. It is vital to point out here that there are boring and unpleasant aspects of all contributions and any paid jobs. Does this mean we don't do the job? No, because as adults we realise that sometimes it is absolutely necessary to do mundane or unpleasant jobs. It's not just tools down because we got a bit bored.

Caregiving roles involve rewarding and boring elements just like any other job.

People have looked me in the eye and said, "Oh, I could never be a stay-at-home mum" with just a touch of disdain. The same way I used to say, "Oh, I'll never be just a housewife". It's really quite offensive to women through the ages who have always worked.

While I have been known to wear a messy bun and track pants, I don't consider myself of lower intellect or less ambitious or lazier than the general population. I had kids and then really saw the value in the day-to-day work of caring for them and being with them. I felt a sense that this wasn't forever, that it was temporary. It's a season and I wanted to lean into it. It's great we have been able to get by financially but it hasn't been comfortable at times. We certainly aren't the only single-income family chewing into savings to support ourselves.

Terms such as 'privilege' and 'luxury' that are used to describe care work also serve to dismiss the importance of the work. We must refrain from referring to unpaid care work as something unattainable and unnecessary. In an ideal world, caring for each other is honoured and supported in policy as a basic human right and we should use language that reflects that if those are the conditions we seek to attain.

Language can also inform our choices by creating forgone conclusions. It's this stigma that had me never want to identify as a SAHM, and therefore fully envisioned I would be a 'working mum'. Then I was super confused when I actually had a baby and didn't identify with either end of the spectrum. Which is another reason labels are so unhelpful – they can pigeonhole people as one or the other. It's really limiting and confusing, especially with something as fluid and dynamic as motherhood.

The phrase 'stay-at-home mum' is a real handbrake on changing cultural perceptions of care work as 'lesser'. The terms 'working mum' and 'SAHM' persist because deep down some women in paid work still want to distinguish themselves from women in unpaid work. They feel like they do more, they have sacrificed more, and that this should be acknowledged. I believe the contributions must be considered different but not 'less than' the other. There are sacrifices and benefits of both contributions. It's only if we don't truly value the work of caring for others that we feel like a mum in paid work is contributing more than a mum in unpaid work, and therefore deserves more support. At the same time, most of us recognise that paid work is pretty much a mini-holiday from the work of caring for little kids all day.

The stigma around the term SAHM influences policy because there is a tendency to see a SAHM as contributing less than a 'working mum', and government is more inclined to fund policy that supports a mum in her paid contribution. For example, we have a $4.7 billion dollar increase in childcare subsidies in the four years up to 2026, but the Federal Government has only just committed to paying superannuation on paid parental leave at a cost of around $200 million dollars annually.

The argument is government can't invest in policies to fund people who are 'essentially doing nothing', but if we started using language more accurately to describe the importance and difficulty of care work then government policy would begin to reflect this.

Once we recognise that our unpaid care work is an equally valuable contribution to society, once we truly assign value to our bodies and ourselves, we may be able to completely do away with the terms SAHM and 'working mum' once and for all. If we really feel the need to make the distinction, we could describe a mum as being in paid or unpaid work. Ultimately, however, if we can arrive at a point where we truly value care work, we may be able to truly embrace and support the contributions of all mothers—in paid or unpaid work—and celebrate each other.

Baby brain

The internet is littered with the sentiment that women become dumb when they become mothers. I'm thinking of one particular reel meme where a guy is explaining a concept by describing putting all the stars in the universe in a hotdog bun. He eventually loses his train of thought and stares into space, unable to draw a reasonable conclusion to the point he was trying to make. The more common manifestation of the idea that mothers are somehow mentally inferior is 'baby brain'.

The 'baby brain' quips have never sat well with me – it's disempowering and infantilising. If anyone else forgets their wallet, it's a minor lapse in memory or focus, but a pregnant woman or new mother[24]? Her brain has turned to mush. Pregnant and postpartum women have been labelled with 'baby brain' for so long it's become part of the lexicon – we don't even realise it's a casual insult deeply rooted in cultural devaluation of care[25]. But recent advances in neuroimaging technology are shattering the age-old baby brain myth[26] with high-resolution images of mothers' brains as incredibly neuroplastic, adaptive and specialised – an updated version of the pre-pregnancy model. Neuroscientists have found pronounced increases in empathy, stress tolerance, creativity, and learning capacity in new mothers.

University of Rennes neuroscientist Jodi Pawluski[27] describes motherhood as a process of finetuning the brain in areas related but not limited to, caregiving. 'The transition to motherhood is marked by some of the most significant changes in brain plasticity in the adult female brain', she wrote in a literature review.

Pawluski argues the science simply does not back up the idea that motherhood is characterised by brain fog and memory deficits. 'The inescapable narrative of "mummy brain" contributes to these subjective reports', she wrote as part of a collaborative essay in

JAMA Neurology earlier this year. 'Objective differences in memory function in mothers have rarely been observed in empirical studies.' The more we circulate this baseless phenomenon, the more women convince themselves of the affliction. Sleep deprivation? Yes. Structural brain deficits? A hard no.

The neurochemistry of pregnancy and childbirth shapes the brain of a mother to strengthen her caregiving abilities, but it's becoming clear there are many applications for these new strengths beyond the nursery. Corporate businesses are increasingly enlisting consultants to deliver the science behind 'mother brain' to the workplace in an effort to better harness the creative potential and new capabilities of mothers returning from maternity leave.

Neuroscientist Dr Jen Hacker Pearson describes her consultancy work with global companies as reframing the way business culture views mothers, but also how mothers view themselves. "A woman returning to the workplace has not been downgraded now she is a mother, but is actually upgraded from a neuroscientific perspective," she explains. "This offers many positives for the company. When mothers are thriving, the world thrives."

Improved brain function in parents makes sense from an evolutionary perspective. If becoming a mother resulted in reduced mental capacity, it would have presented a real threat to offspring survival and the future of the human population. The challenges presented by parenthood through the ages have long demanded creativity or extra mental and physical resources. Adoptive parents, partners who haven't given birth, and relatives closely involved in caregiving also experience similar brain changes, though not to the same extent as birth mothers.

Emerging research also shows the mother-brain changes are far more enduring than initially thought, with a study published in *Brain Sciences 2021* demonstrating an ability to determine if a woman was a mother with over 90% accuracy simply by looking at brain scans at six-years postpartum. In 2020, a Monash University Cognitive Imaging team found motherhood has a neuroprotective effect later in life. In the study, elderly women with more children showed patterns of brain activity in the opposite direction to age-related decline. The benefits appear to be obtained through the way motherhood provides lifelong environmental complexity and novel challenges associated with raising children through developmental stages.

If the science exploring the way motherhood changes a woman's brain for the better has come as a complete surprise to you, you're not the only one. Research in this area is woefully under-reported because it undermines the 'sameness equality' agendas that rely on women being the same as men in order to be considered equal. Scientific research that proves pregnancy and birth increases a woman's aptitude for caring for an infant, both physically and psychologically, is directly at odds with dominant feminist ideologies that seek to distance women from their roles as mothers.

After a flurry of peer-reviewed research articles beginning at the turn of the millennium, citing the brain plasticity—'rejuvenation' and 'neurogenesis' being observed in mothers' brains—we can be left in no doubt that 'baby brain' is a deeply inaccurate term. So why does it persist?

The baby-brain rhetoric was initially used to reinforce beliefs that women didn't belong in the workplace or certain professions because they had inferior mental capacity. It is still in the interests of misogynistic quarters to perpetuate these ideas. But now that most reasonable people recognise the value of women in the workplace, the dated baby-brain myth seems to have taken on a new function of devaluing motherhood or warning women off staying in motherland for too long.

The persistence of the term could be traced back to misinterpretations of research that showed reduced grey matter in the brains of pregnant and postpartum women. Reductions in grey matter are usually associated with cognitive decline and degenerative conditions such as dementia, but in pregnancy it is considered to strengthen certain skills and prime the brain for rapid growth in the immediate postpartum period.

The grey-matter findings were initially weaponised to reinforce baby-brain rhetoric but Elseline Hoekzema, a researcher at Leiden University in the Netherlands, told *The New York Times* that grey-matter loss can be advantageous. "It can also represent a beneficial process of maturation or specialisation".

It could be that the research that has uncovered the inaccuracy of the term 'baby brain' is still relatively new, evolving and yet to permeate cultural perceptions of motherhood. The baby-brain myth is still perpetuated by many in the medical community. Emerging neuroscience need not relegate women to realms of domesticity but rather could be used to justify policies and workplace legislation that recognise the unique role of mothers in caregiving. The neuroscience and research also provides clear justification for increased supports for mothers by demonstrating increased vulnerability to mental illness. While motherhood is a time of significant cognitive potential, a brain in a constant state of change is also particularly vulnerable to forming maladaptive neural pathways.

The misconception that pregnant women and new mothers have lower brain function has, to some extent, been internalised and perpetuated by mothers themselves. Even with my particular aversion to the term, I have found myself on occasion muttering "must be baby brain" to explain a forgotten appointment.

The unfounded and pervasive belief in 'baby brain' may inhibit a mother's ability to regain confidence in public or paid-work settings. It leads to a sense that care work causes lower brain function and that the work of caring for children should be avoided to regain intellectual function. It contributes to the stigma associated with caregiving roles, that they are for less-intellectual types.

Far from dumbing down, the experience of becoming a parent has been expansive and cerebral. I am aware of a new dimension to my thinking, an edge to my creativity, and a certain boldness when it comes to doing what needs to be done. I find myself questioning everything and seeing it anew.

Misplaced misery

We need to identify and limit language that suggests mothers in unpaid work are somehow unfulfilled or not contributing in the best possible way. We see this in the media often with terms like caregiving being a 'burden' or 'holding women back' or even 'clipping our wings'. This language has its roots in the sad, alcoholic-housewife narrative of the 1950s, which denigrated the role of caregiving but also I think misplaced the source of the housewives' misery.

It's not that the work of raising our kids isn't meaningful; housewives in the '50s were doing valuable and meaningful work, but laws that prevented them from working meant they lacked choice and agency and were disconnected from power and influence.

Correctly identifying the source of the discontent—being unsupported, lonely, and alienated rather than being unfulfilled— and adjusting language to better reflect this will go a long way to improving cultural perceptions of care. Care work can be boring, but aren't all jobs boring at some point? The thing that makes jobs stimulating is connection with others, finding meaning in our work, and feeling valued. An ecologist might get bored by the end of a long day counting beetles in a 20-metre-square quadrant. The sun might be hot and their colleague might be super annoying, but because they are measuring the effect of environmental rehabilitation procedures, they keep going. Also, they are getting paid and they know they get to knock off at some point.

We can even do work that is kind of meaningless if we have a great team of colleagues and we are paid fairly and get to go home at the end of the day. The thing that makes a job truly soul destroying is if we don't feel valued, we are overworked and/or we don't get paid enough – sounds like motherhood.

Its redeeming factor is that IT IS meaningful work *and* important, but this isn't well recognised. Poor working conditions of motherhood can rob us of the enjoyment of it and leave us vulnerable to poor mental health.

The SAHM role seems to be a perfect storm for many – unpaid, unsupported, and unseen. The decision to return to a paid role in some capacity seems like a natural response to this scenario. But let's stop saying it's because unpaid care work is boring or unfulfilling. Enabling women to enter paid work when they choose is critical, but this doesn't solve the root cause of the distress for so many. This doesn't result in true freedom of choice and truly valuing both paid and unpaid contributions.

Valuing paid care work, too

As long as we constantly frame caregiving as something to be 'liberated' from, something that 'holds women back', we cannot expect this work to be truly valued in either a paid or an unpaid capacity. We lament the fact that so many Australian women are so well educated and then end up raising their own children like it's a massive waste of everyone's time. Then we turn around and expect our best and brightest to flock to the childcare sector?

Overhauling the language around care more broadly will also have positive policy implications in the paid care-work sector. Cultural shifts in this space will be more successful if they come from a deep sense of value of all care in this space. Continuing to use demeaning and dismissive language around unpaid care in relation to mothers, also actually undermines attempts to improve conditions for early educators.

If we don't truly challenge the language and internalised beliefs that arise from this, if care work is 'doing nothing', why is high-quality childcare so important? If care work is doing nothing, why is it so important that educators are qualified and have good working conditions? Progress in valuing paid care sectors is held back because deep cultural devaluation remains.

Tradwife saga

Google search trends show searches for tradwife—derived from the phrase 'traditional housewife'—began ramping up in 2018 in line with the rise of Instagram influencers role-playing as traditional housewives[28]. They dress up in vintage clothes, make food from scratch, and care for their children. The aesthetic they create ranges from saccharine through idyllic to satire. Sometimes, they are religiously motivated; others have breadwinner husbands who 'lead the household'; and others still have opted out of contraception.

I'm calling it role-playing because these women do not find themselves in the original set of circumstances that led to many traditional housewives having no genuine choice, such as no access to contraception, little education, and no prospects other than child-bearing and homemaking.

Tradwives emulate certain romantic features of this existence by choice and without the harmful reality of necessity, scarcity, and oppression. The tradwife trend is a protest against hustle culture and modern expectations that women will run back to the office a few weeks after giving birth so they can start to be productive again. They rebel against fast food, commercialised care, mass-produced rubbish, and rushed days.

Feminists were alarmed by the sheer number of followers these women attracted. After so carefully and painstakingly constructing the narrative that housewives were sad, unfulfilled, backward, and unnecessary, the tradwives shot it to pieces overnight with their intelligence, professional accomplishments, seriously handy skills and, god forbid, their happiness in looking after their kids.

Tradwives hit a nerve with feminists because they directly challenge the idea of career women as the gold standard. Caregivers rarely, if ever, have been able to publicise themselves in the same way career women could. Until now. Before tradwives, caregivers and movements that sought to include them in women's liberation struggled to curry favour with the public because care work and unpaid labour have an image problem. It's not glamorous work. It's laborious and messy and often lonely, invisible work. It doesn't pay the big bucks and it goes on in private.

Before the age of social media, the likes of Martha Stewart and Nigella Lawson—the latter of whom popularised the term 'domestic goddess'—made their fortunes through giving womanhood and homemaking broad marketing appeal. Tradwives are kind of like the Martha Stewarts of social media – a bunch of women with undeniable business acumen who knew they could monetise their image and tear down the tired housewife perceptions in an instant.

Tradwives are disingenuous, of course, but so is everyone posting on social media. So are the women who pose as effortlessly 'having it all' while battling the emotional and physical turmoil of juggling paid work with carrying, birthing, and rearing children. There are countless career women on social media guilty of virtue signalling and sharing the minutiae of their day-to-day lives. All that has changed is that housewives decided to do it too.

Feminists realised they needed to turn public favour against tradwives and position them as the new bogeyman – the enemy of modern women. The term traditional wife, what tradwives occasionally had called themselves, sounded too distinguished, so it was truncated to tradwife. We know this change in terminology did not originate with tradwives themselves because they rarely, if ever, refer to themselves as tradwives.

Mainstream media outlets and women's media platforms have been absolutely committed to making sure the tradwife label sticks. This makes sense because the media obviously is over-represented by women who are actively engaged in careers and are likely ideologically opposed to tradwives. The articles describe the tradwives as 'self-harm for millennial mothers', cult-like, and victims of oppression and abuse.

Mainstream feminism is seeking to take back control of the housewife narrative by repackaging women who work in the home by choice as representative of something dangerous. They argue that tradwives 'romanticise oppression', are victims of internalised oppression and are setting a dangerous example for young girls. They argue every which way that any woman in her right mind wouldn't actually choose this. They dangle tradwives threateningly as what could happen if women let their guard down and assume caregiving roles.

Perhaps the biggest and most recent take-down of a tradwife was mounted by reporter Megan Agnew in *The Times*. Agnew visited Hannah Neeleman—known as the 'queen of the tradwives' because of her almost 10 million Instagram followers—her husband Daniel and their eight children on Ballerina Farm in Utah. The reporter claimed to have witnessed certain dynamics—after spending all of a single day with the family—that concerned her. Based on her own apparent spidey senses, Agnew set about framing Neeleman as a sad victim of coercive control and 'baby trapping'.

The quotes in the article fail to support Agnew's conclusions, but it's obvious to any reader that Agnew's agenda was decided before she set foot in Neeleman's home. Her preconceived ideas about caregivers and housewives prevented her from seeing Neeleman's life as a choice. She deliberately reduced Neeleman to an overworked, unhappy wife dominated by her husband, apparently regardless of what Neeleman actually said, because that's the only image of mothers in the home that Agnew is interested in creating.

Neeleman herself later flatly denied the claims in the profile, but many women seem deaf to her. It's a stark example of tradwives being oppressed only by other women.

Feminists are right to argue that tradwives are promoting a choice that would render most women vulnerable and financially insecure. However, the problem isn't actually women and the work they do, it's how this work is viewed and supported by society. The problem is lack of paid leave, work flexibility, and carer-support measures. Instead of fighting for societal change and policy that would better support unpaid care work and labour, feminists remain focused on problematising women such as tradwives and their choices.

The same women who are up in arms about wealthy tradwives also conveniently ignore the elitist elements of career women. Middle- and low-income families often do not have the same luxuries as high-income families who can pick and choose high-quality, boutique childcare centres or take advantage of generous parental leave packages in their high-paying jobs. They promote a choice in which they are buffered from the pitfalls.

For the record, I am not a tradwife. The only time I want my husband to lead me is if I have failing sight. I'd love some freshly baked bread if someone else could be in charge of that. Contraception is absolutely critical at this point for our family and I can't bring myself to wear an apron. I'll gradually increase my paid work hours as I see fit. I don't have a name for what goes on in our house and my role in it, but it has been great and it has been my choice. I'd wish that for anyone, including the tradwives.

I may not be a tradwife but I have been called one in wholesale attempts to undermine my ideas, identity, and character. The term is being weaponised against everyday caregivers for doing something as simple as growing veggies or baking muffins. Caregivers who are called tradwives out of spite often then wrongly assume the identity and unwittingly perpetuate the campaign to ridicule and dismiss work in the home.

The definition is slowly expanding to include a much larger subset of caregivers than the original handful of social-media personalities in unique circumstances. Girls growing up today will likely recoil at the possibility of being labelled a tradwife if they take extended parental leave or engage in caregiving on a long-term basis.

The tradwife episode just proves that some women will stop at nothing to find novel ways to tear down mothers who work inside the home. We continue to be our own worst enemy.

Shifting our internalised beliefs

People who use derogatory language often aren't intending to denigrate unpaid caregivers – they just have such a deeply internalised devaluation of care that they don't realise they are doing it. They also have difficulty imagining care work being a valued, prioritised, and worthy role. They assume people in caregiving roles have 'had their wings clipped'. Changing the language we use in relation to caregivers on a surface level allows us to actively challenge internalised beliefs we hold about care work.

Internalised beliefs are tricky to pinpoint sometimes because they can become part of our nature and are often subconsciously held; we go through most of our lives unaware of the ways we have diminished the work of care and those who do it. It can be as simple as the belief that care work is for weak, unambitious, or less educated people. That you have to be soft and nurturing and motherly in nature to excel as a caregiver. It's only until we actively force ourselves to notice the effort, strength, and mental endurance required of caregivers that we begin to understand the flaws in our assumptions.

The reason caregivers often feel so frustrated in their role is because they have internalised beliefs that this work is easy and is carried out by motherly-types who enjoy every moment and peacefully knead dough at the kitchen bench. When we find ourselves immersed in work that is anything but easy, while still holding the assumption that it should be easy, we feel like we have failed. We feel frustrated and angry that it's not what we assumed it to be. But unless we challenge and change our deepest beliefs, we will continue in this state of chronic and uncomfortable misalignment.

Changing internalised beliefs requires effort to think critically about our own thought processes and challenging why our expectations are not lining up with reality. Is it because the reality is not normal? Or because our expectation is not realistic? If our expectations are often unmet, it's likely we are holding some internalised belief that assumes a different scenario than the reality we are experiencing. A basic example of changing an internalised belief goes like this:

1. We hold the internalised belief that breastfeeding is easy.

2. We engage in enough breastfeeding to experience the reality of breastfeeding not being easy.

3. Instead of continuing to be frustrated, angry, and sad at ourselves for not being able to easily breastfeed, we start to change our belief that breastfeeding is easy.

4. The next time we experience a cluster feed or feel over stimulated while breastfeeding, we are less angry and frustrated because we recognise that breastfeeding can be difficult.

5. We will still have a reflex to be frustrated about the time-consuming and difficult nature of breastfeeding, but these

moments become fewer and are often followed by our new belief that this is normal.

6. Because we recognise that breastfeeding can be difficult, we organise support and ask for help that better reflects the degree of difficulty and the value of our time and skill invested in breastfeeding.

7. Because internalised beliefs are so enduring, the reflex to feel frustrated by breastfeeding may never completely go away or it may still arise every now and again even once we find it natural and easy.

This scenario can be applied to almost every aspect of care, and is often identified by mothers as 'lowering expectations' but it's really a process of challenging and changing internalised beliefs that care work was easy, natural, effortless, and enjoyable all the time. Thinking we should be able to get out of the house easily and quickly, expecting we will be able to keep our cool, assuming it will be easy to cook for everyone and keep up with the housework. We have the belief that cleaning is easy because cleaning is a lower paid and less respected job, but in reality it is hard and constant work. When we suck at it, we get down on ourselves because we have an internalised belief that domestic work is easy or a job requiring fewer skills. In reality, domestic work is a skill and it is hard labour that has really only been devalued because mostly women do it.

Care is a different kind of intelligence that we can't learn in school. A lot of A-type personalities who have experienced success and achievement struggle especially when they are an amateur, and are having to start from scratch building skills and operating in grey areas where we don't have clear indicators or metrics to measure our performance.

Another way to challenge internalised beliefs around care work is to recognise that care work has for centuries been carried out by the physically strongest and mentally toughest among us. Without the strength and endurance of caregivers and mothers, we simply could not have evolved. Only the strongest could survive the physical and mental strain of raising dependents with the longest infancy in the animal kingdom.

Value of caregiving reflected in society

Once we change our language and challenge internalised beliefs, we should start to see people who actually assign value to women and care work making their way into positions of power and influence. This new generation of leaders should theoretically then make decisions that reflect the actual value of caregiving and the support it requires. Policies (we will come to these in more detail later) that treat care work as a legitimate and vital contribution act as positive feedback for caregivers. Parents reason that if this contribution is supported and respected in government policy, it must be a worthy and legitimate contribution. Thus, caregivers would not only have material support, but they would also feel more valued and derive more fulfillment.

Public-sector innovations and improvements to workplace culture and attitudes to caregivers also force private sectors to improve attitudes to caregivers. When private sectors introduce work flexibility, options for reduced hours and parental leave packages, it sends the message that people who have care responsibilities are valued. Workplaces understand that caregivers bring a unique perspective and skill-set to any workplace. We must not treat people with care responsibilities as though they are a liability or a less valued member of the team. It is a reality of society that at any given time many (perhaps most) people in a paid workplace will have care responsibilities outside of the paid workplace.

In addition, properly valuing care work would lead to more willingness from government to legislate pay increases and improve work conditions in the paid care-work sector, which will in turn raise the status of unpaid care work by association.

CHAPTER SIX

Pregnancy and Postpartum

I first lost control of my bladder while sprinting about six months after the birth of my second baby. I had no idea how to safely return to exercise after childbirth. Since the birth of our first baby ended up in an emergency caesarean section, symptoms of damage to my pelvic floor didn't appear until after the second birth, which was the first vaginal birth. In 2018, I opted for an induction due to early symptoms of preeclampsia being detected and my history of uncontrollable blood pressure in late-term pregnancy. I laboured as long as I could before opting for an epidural and eventually delivering on my back, being told to push through my bottom and no sensation of what would constitute effective pushing. In the end, I had an episiotomy and required forceps to deliver my daughter, who had part of the umbilical cord wrapped several times around her neck. I was anaemic and exhausted afterwards, requiring a wheelchair to get back to the ward even though sensation had returned to my legs.

Several years later, I would learn that my first vaginal delivery was a recipe for pelvic floor disaster, but at the time nothing was mentioned about rehab beyond 'make sure you do your kegels'. I did do my kegels but thought this was for the purpose of simply being able to control my bladder, not rehabilitating the muscle that was holding up all my pelvic organs. I had zero awareness of what rehabilitation involved. My episiotomy stitches fell out two days after delivery and the decision was made to leave the incision to heal without stitches.

I didn't wet my pants often, only in moments of full exertion and fatigue. I also discovered I could no longer jump on the trampoline due to the feeling of internal heaviness with each spring. So, I simply decided I could live without trampoline jumping, and I might have to ease up on the sprints.

Looking back, it's incredible how easily I dismissed these significant physiological changes, even if they weren't super noticeable at first. I also had issues with bowel movements, which I did not know were related to childbirth injuries. It was only five years after my symptoms first appeared that I realised I needed serious pelvic-floor rehabilitation – about six months after the birth of my fourth and last child.

My lack of awareness around the changes I experienced can, in part, be put down to the fact that women's experiences of pelvic-floor issues are seldom talked about. Many women accept the changes to their body as normal and unable to be addressed. On some level, I was embarrassed and ashamed that the toilet situation had changed. It wasn't until two close friends of mine experienced prolapses that I ever really heard the issues being talked about. I finally recognised my own symptoms for what they were – preventable and treatable pelvic-floor weakness that I had unwittingly worsened.

I was in denial that childbirth could have such a huge impact on my body. I wanted so badly to 'bounce back' and return to doing all the work I was previously doing. In this sense, I see myself as a product of a society that conditions us to not really respect or honour postpartum, and this extends into motherhood and other caregiving experiences.

Because postpartum is viewed as a liability in paid-work conditions, this period has been extensively minimised, downplayed, and hidden in order to ensure women were able to take up paid jobs as soon as possible. As a 'career girlie', I 100% subscribed to this view of postpartum and didn't want to be seen as weakened by the process of childbirth.

I also noticed dismissive attitudes toward postpartum recovery within the healthcare sector itself. The focus was very much on pregnancy and birth and everyone quickly lost interest after that. Midwives and doctors wanted to look at my vagina quite often before the baby was born, but I had to beg healthcare professionals to inspect my episiotomy wound after the birth. It was this reluctance to actually look at my vagina that led to inadequate post-delivery care.

Beyond the initial period of episiotomy recovery—a procedure I had with my first vaginal birth because it was hospital policy to perform an episiotomy when forceps were used—what little dialogue there had been between myself and healthcare providers on this issue completely faded. I kind of gave up and, sadly, in Australia referral to women's health physio is not a routine part of postpartum care. This is shocking considering three in four women will experience some degree of pelvic organ prolapse. Around 50% of women will experience incontinence issues.

The failures went both ways – I couldn't identify warning signs and didn't ask the right questions, but also the postpartum screening processes failed to pick up the need for pelvic-floor physiotherapy while it picked up physio treatments for other conditions like abdominal separation.

I had known early on that incontinence was related to pelvic-floor weakness as this was mentioned in antenatal classes and by midwives following each birth. I did do some sporadic Pilates following the incident when I lost control of my bladder but with no medical background, I didn't properly understand the importance of how the pelvic floor functioned. I was never informed about how the episiotomy could also affect pelvic-floor function. I remember my shock upon learning the pelvic-floor muscle was holding up all the organs within the pelvis so that the bowel, vaginal canal, and bladder could properly function. Because the only warning sign flagged with me was urinary incontinence, and I could still hold a pee under normal circumstances, I didn't prioritise my pelvic-floor health particularly as the care work I was performing increased and overwhelm set in.

Postpartum health issues were previously taken very seriously, particularly where people only had access to rudimentary medical treatments, if any at all. Historically, postpartum women from different cultures and varying social classes all over the world have undergone postpartum periods of rest with the baby in order to properly heal and prevent health issues. This is still a common practice in developing nations where access to healthcare is poor and the population relies heavily on prevention. It also still remains common practice in Eastern cultures.

In *The Golden Month*, postpartum researcher Jenny Allison, explores the decline of these practices, particularly in Western societies and the negative health impacts that have resulted. Postpartum recoveries began to be minimised as birthing moved out of the home and into the hospital domain, but also as modern medicine dramatically reduced the infant-maternal mortality rate. Then in more recent decades, postpartum recoveries were further eroded in order to facilitate earlier returns to paid work and increased paid workforce participation for women. Throughout history, there are examples of social inequality in postpartum care where very poor mothers may be forced to return to paid labour soon after birth. However, postpartum care rituals were often common practice across social classes, even for the very poor, and in a variety of different cultural settings.

Evidence of the reduction in postpartum care in recent decades is most clearly observed in the Australian hospital system. In the 1950s it was common for a new mother to remain in hospital for up to two weeks following the birth of a child, while today we see the postpartum hospital stay reduced to 24-48 hours.

In the Western and developed world today, we see a gross minimisation of pregnancy, childbirth, and the postpartum period to the detriment of women's health and wellbeing. We compensate for this by increasing medicalisation and reactive healthcare, even though preventative solutions are cheaper and more effective.

Women are largely also expected to attend to all their usual paid and unpaid commitments during pregnancy. This is despite up to 90% of women experiencing nausea and vomiting during pregnancy[29], which can be debilitating and result in extreme fatigue levels.

Research also now shows that a pregnant woman's body operates at the peak threshold of long-term human endurance. In 2019, a study found that during pregnancy a woman's body remains at more than double the normal resting metabolic rate[30]. To put this in context, a person doing a three-month trek through Antarctica sits at around 3.5 times the resting metabolic rate.

Childbirth itself results in huge energy expenditure and pushes most normal pain thresholds to the limit. A woman's skeletal structure will shift significantly to accommodate the baby, so much so that childbirth can actually break a tailbone in a small percentage of births. Tearing of skin and tissue in and around the vagina is common. Childbirth can result in major surgery.

Around one third of all women who have given birth in Australia report that they have experienced birth trauma[31]. In 2024, for the first time ever, a parliamentary committee investigated and reported on birth trauma in Australia, finding unacceptably high levels of obstetric violence and PTSD following births. It also found the ripple effects of difficult and traumatic births extended well into the postpartum period, a time during which the World Health Organisation (WHO) notes that three in ten women receive inadequate care. The recommendations centred on prevention of birth trauma but also focused on overhauling the postpartum period with better screening processes and post-birth services to address a range of mental and physical issues.

The Birth Trauma Inquiry was a promising step towards undoing the minimisation and dismissive attitudes towards pregnancy, birth, and postpartum periods. It recognised these are huge transitions for women to undergo – healthcare systems, policies, and cultural attitudes must shift to reflect this.

Women may have long-term or lifelong birth injuries, but postpartum recovery in terms of hormones and muscle elasticity and skeletal structure settling back into a normal position usually takes between two and seven years. Around 40% of all women are living with a degree of prolapse[32]. And yet one in four mothers in the US return to paid work at just two weeks postpartum. Data from the 2018 census in Australia showed that 42% of women had returned to work since the birth of their youngest child. Of these women, 74% returned after four months at home with their child, up from 65% in 2011.

Childbirth is also an extraordinary psychological transition, that in less than ideal conditions can result in psychological injury and long-term mental illness struggles. A significant percentage of women will experience postpartum anxiety and depression, PTSD, and psychosis. At the 2024 NSW Inquiry into Birth Trauma, consumer group Maternity Choices Australia reported that one-in-four mothers develop postnatal depression, and one-in-ten have post-traumatic stress disorder[33].

Childbirth has huge physical and mental implications for women. Even a completely uncomplicated pregnancy, delivery, and postpartum period is still an enormous transformation for a woman to undergo and will require time and support to fully recover. Yet support for a healthy and well-rested pregnancy, evidence-based and trauma-informed hospital practice, and postpartum rest and care remain woefully underfunded and unexplored worldwide. Policies and cultural attitudes that could reduce or eliminate many of the difficulties women face are still largely absent from the conversation.

Our reluctance to address these issues is, in part, due to the fact that pregnancy, birth, and postpartum are largely irreconcilable within dominant equality theory – equality as 'sameness', because these experiences are almost always impossible for women to reduce or avoid. These are what we might consider 'fixed' parts of the female experience that are unable to be addressed by strategies to reduce women's disadvantage by enabling them to be more like men.

The dominant equality-as-sameness strategy relies on women being enabled to reduce or minimise their disadvantage, for example by outsourcing childcare. It is not only extremely difficult to translate outsourcing models to pregnancy and childbirth contexts, but also undesirable and inhumane, as it has the potential to commodify women's reproductive labour in a way that results in further harm to lower-socioeconomic women.

In this sense, equality-as-sameness governing principles could be seen as largely responsible for falling birth rates and the economic problems that come with that. Women reduce their financial disadvantage and vulnerability by having fewer children.

By continuing to minimise pregnancy, childbirth, and recovery, we have inadvertently limited the visibility of these human processes, and thereby reduced the ability of society and policy makers to respond and support women. Even today, many governments and workplaces continue to pursue policy that simply enables women to avoid care work rather than valuing and including that work as an indispensable societal function.

If pregnancy, childbirth, and recovery is 'no big deal' and the work of 'caring for children' simply drudgery that is beneath women, if our only dignity is to be found in paid work, then the social support for these care functions is naturally reduced. Scarcity in support networks doesn't just affect our postpartum experience, the impacts of this lack of support begin in pregnancy. Research has shown a mother's perception of her available support networks can impact her mental health and feelings around the birth[34].

The lack of visibility of mothering also greatly reduces a woman's exposure to natural processes of breastfeeding and general infant nurturing. We attempt to make up for this lack of exposure through formal instruction such as antenatal programs and birthing classes, but it's a poor substitute for the real-life incidental and organic exposure. Many women report dissatisfaction with formal antenatal education. Women are still heading in to childbirth with a general sense of under-preparedness, but also *actual* under-preparedness.

While we may never be able to replicate the real-life childbirth and baby-care exposure that would have been possible in tribal and communal-living settings, nor may we want to, we must still acknowledge this lack of preparedness. We must work to offer more holistic, extensive antenatal support. We can explore programs that create real-life exposure to parenthood, such as 'Manma' in Japan where a network of host families across the country welcome young people who are interested in parenting into their home to experience a realistic day in the life of a parent. Hinae Nori founded the organisation in 2013 as a way of addressing concerns young people had about under-preparedness as well as the financial burden of raising children or balancing work and family life. "Playing with children, and openly discussing their worries and uncertainties with experienced parents can help young people gain the confidence to build a family, ultimately recognizing the deep value of family and feeling assured in their ability to raise a child."

The more we empower and respect reproductive labour, the more visible women and caregivers become and the easier it is to share information about this period and disseminate through the community. Parents should be considered a source of knowledge and skills to be shared with younger people in the community rather than a liability who are forced to hide their childcare responsibilities. If women are hiding their postpartum pains so they can be taken seriously at paid work, important conversations that highlight these issues will be less forthcoming.

Increasing the visibility and importance of appropriate postpartum care also means it is more likely to attract government funding. Investing in antenatal and postnatal care has been shown time and again to improve health outcomes of women and children. Investments in the earliest years—including from pre-conception health of couples trying to conceive—pay large dividends in the form of reducing costly interventions later in life.

Antenatal classes should be well resourced and delivered by health professionals with adequate support and training. Antenatal care must offer support for physical care during pregnancy—for example, support to lower smoking while pregnant—but also go beyond the birth and include information on how to care for a mother and baby, how to breastfeed, realistic recovery times, and how to access support services. Antenatal women's health physio is becoming increasingly common practice but subsidised antenatal physio will be essential to ensuring all women access this care.

It is not abnormal for a woman to require intensive support for many weeks, if not months, postpartum, but adequate recovery times are rarely afforded. Lying down in the postpartum period is a key measure used to promote proper healing of the pelvic organs, which can prevent prolapse. High rates of prolapse and continence issues in the general population of mothers[35] is a direct result of inadequate postpartum rest times and preventative care. The French government has responded to this issue by introducing 10 free sessions with a pelvic-health professional for mothers who have recently given birth[36]. A similar model could be introduced here to prevent prolapse, reduce the need for expensive surgical intervention, and improve quality of life for women who are already experiencing symptoms.

The importance of postpartum recovery is reflected in the fact that many cultures still provide intensive support for up to 60 days postpartum or longer if required. An extended model of intensive care for mothers during the postpartum period is in stark contrast to the current hospital system and cultural-care expectations in many Western nations. Most Australian hospitals encourage a short postpartum stay for just a couple of days before heading home to care for a new baby – mostly unassisted and often alone. This is undoubtedly a result of underfunded maternity services.

As much as some mothers may feel more comfortable in the home environment, there are many who return home before they feel ready. Given that up to one third of mothers describe their birth experience as traumatic, as well as the changing hormone levels and challenges of learning how to care for a baby, we know that postpartum periods can be an extremely vulnerable time in a mental-health sense[37]. Optional, longer hospital stays could be an extended opportunity for easy and supported access to psychological services, breastfeeding assistance, or general baby-care assistance.

Postnatal depression is higher in women who lack support and who are forced to return to work before they are ready. Jessica Shortall explained in a TED Talk titled 'The American Case for Paid Maternity Leave', "Statistically speaking, the shorter a woman's leave after having a baby, the more likely she will be to suffer from postpartum mood disorders like postpartum depression and anxiety.

And among many potential consequences of those disorders, suicide is the second most common cause of death in a woman's first year postpartum."

Returning to paid work is often a recommended treatment for postnatal depression. Rather than addressing the systemic lack of support for mothers and how this can lead to mental illness, or helping a mother feel validated and capable in her caregiving role, we literally treat a psychological illness with more work for a mother and separation from her baby. To treat the primary cause of postnatal mental illness, more support is desperately needed in the form of home visits from or access to family, friends, and health professionals. Direct instruction is required in some cases but also physical support in the home to allow a woman to focus on caring for her baby and learning to breastfeed rather than keeping up with domestic duties or returning to paid work. Support that allows a mother to feel rested and gather strength to overcome the challenges of a new baby is critical.

Low breastfeeding rates are one of the most obvious indicators that postpartum support is inadequate. The World Health Organisation states that less than half of the world's infants are breastfed for the first six months in a report released in 2019, which urged governments around the world to implement policies that facilitated breastfeeding[38]. Upper middle-income countries like Australia have some of the lowest breastfeeding rates worldwide, with just 24% of babies exclusively breastfed up to six months, down from 29% in 2012.

Given the evidence-based benefits of breastfeeding for mother and baby, the fact that breastfeeding continues to be minimised by government policy and workplaces is a shocking failure. The physical act of breastfeeding is directly at odds with returning to paid work and leaving proximity of the baby in early years, yet inadequate paid parental leave persists around the world.

The WHO recommends breastfeeding for two years and beyond because of significant health benefits for babies with reduced risk of gastrointestinal infections, eczema, asthma, middle ear infections, urinary tract infections, and respiratory infections. They are also less likely to become obese, develop some childhood cancers, type 1 or 2 diabetes and are less likely to die from SIDS. When breastfed babies do get sick they are less likely to be hospitalised.

Breastfeeding has also been shown to be a protective factor against the mother developing postnatal mental illness[39]. It assists the uterus to return to its pre-pregnant state faster, can help women return to a healthy weight range, and reduces the risk of ovarian cancer and pre-menopausal breast cancer[40].

Breastfeeding is often seen as a barrier to gender equality, with some going as far as to say that bottle feeding is the only way to achieve equality. The benefits of breastfeeding are well-established and compelling. Breastfeeding is a key reason for longer paid parental leave, yet often the benefits are downplayed or even denied in service of the idea that women should be in paid work as soon as possible after childbirth.

The other reason benefits of breastfeeding are downplayed is to protect women's feelings when breastfeeding hasn't been possible and they feel a sense of failure or sadness. Rather than creating conditions where women might have adequate support to breastfeed, or addressing the factors that can lead to breastfeeding issues such as separation at birth, the solution has been to deny that there is much of a reason to breastfeed.

Awareness of breastfeeding benefits is also drowned out by well-resourced infant formula companies that have been very successful in creating an image that formula is positive, necessary, and beneficial. We know there are definite public health cost savings associated with extended breastfeeding periods, but there is little money to be made—no money exchanging hands—through promoting breastfeeding. Formula feeding is better for the GDP and in the context of economic productivity being the absolute priority, it is difficult to sustain movements to compete with that.

In 2023, medical science journal *The Lancet* released an extensive series of articles on the complex predatory tactics used by formula companies[41]. The articles exposed how formula companies continue to violate international codes introduced specifically to stop industry lobbying governments and misinforming parents in order to increase sales. Perhaps one of the most concerning tactics highlighted in the series was the role of formula companies in actively lobbying against paid parental leave policy. "Some CMF [commercial milk formula] lobby groups have cautioned against improved parental leave. Duration of paid maternity leave is correlated with breastfeeding prevalence and duration, and absence of, or inadequate, paid leave forces many mothers to return to work soon after childbirth. Lack of safe spaces for breastfeeding or expressing milk in workplaces, or facilities to store breastmilk, mean that breastfeeding is not a viable option for many women."

A more insidious tactic linked to the formula industry is the use of gender politics to promote sales. For example, by framing breastfeeding advocacy as a moralistic judgement of mothers who cannot or choose not to breastfeed. Attempts to draw on evidence are positioned as anti-feminist and harmful to women while milk formula is framed as inclusive and empowering. It's a real-time example of how minimising the benefits of breastfeeding and actively reducing support for it can and does play out. A similar pattern emerges when we look at the childcare industry, though we will come to this later in the book. Parent care is less profitable for the childcare industry, which actively minimises the importance for parent care and, in doing so, both directly and indirectly reduces support for parents caring for children at home.

In terms of solutions, we addressed ways to shift cultural attitudes at an individual level earlier in the book. We have looked at policy solutions that could also both inform attitudes and offer practical support. But there are also market-based solutions that could better support breastfeeding and the postpartum period. The Australian National University's Green Feeding Tool was designed to help governments measure breastfeeding rates as a carbon offset[42]. It's leading research on how behavioural modifications could form part of our Long-Term Emissions Reduction Plan.

It's a new chapter in improving our climate response, public health, and support systems for new mothers[43] in one fell swoop. You can go to the website right now, enter the details on how long you have breastfed and the tool gives you a figure on how much carbon has been offset but also puts a dollar value on your milk. It highlights that breastfeeding mothers are lower emitters, with milk travelling only a few metres to reach the baby in the house. Cows' milk must travel from farm to factory, where it undergoes energy and water-intensive processing to produce powdered-milk formula. It is then distributed right around the globe, travelling thousands of kilometres to countries with low rates of breastfeeding. The formula must then be warmed in bottles that are sterilised, usually with heat, over and over again.

According to the algorithms developed by ANU Honorary Associate Professor, Julie Smith, my breastfeeding efforts are enough to offset greenhouse gas emissions from the use of our family car for one year. It's a bigger carbon offset than going vegan for eighteen months or vegetarian for two and half years. It also easily offsets 144kg of greenhouse gas emissions resulting from an estimated 36kg of formula we used after weaning.

Of course, this issue is emblematic of a wider problem with emissions-intensive food production systems. Behavioural modifications such as veganism and sustainable dietary choices are undoubtedly on the rise. We seem willing to respond to the evidence when it comes to adult food choices but not when it comes to infant nutrition.

The positive impacts of improving rates of breastfeeding are difficult to ignore. Research from the World Health Organisation estimates that exclusively breastfeeding all babies in Britain for the first six months would offset the use of up to 77,000 cars every year.

Smith has also attempted to quantify cost savings in the public health system achieved through the optimal infant nutrition breastmilk provides. Using data from her 2002 study based on early weaning at Canberra Hospital, Smith estimates that improving breastfeeding rates could save up to $120m each year across the Australian hospital system. A study from the US showed breastfed babies presented at hospital less and required fewer prescriptions. The federal Department of Health cites evidence showing breastfeeding reduces rates of gastroenteritis, ear and respiratory infections in babies, as well as reducing chronic health issues such as obesity, cancer, and diabetes for both mother and baby across a lifetime. Considering the federal cost-burden of obesity is $11.8bn, even a small reduction in obesity rates equates to a substantial cost saving.

This compelling case was made to a parliamentary inquiry into breastfeeding 2007. The committee recommended the development of a national strategy to improve breastfeeding rates but it failed to reverse a long-term steady decline. In Australia today only 15% of babies are exclusively breastfed by six months, compared with 18% in 2001. We are well below the global average of 44%, and not even close to the Australian Dietary Guidelines aim of 80% by 2013.

A renewed National Breastfeeding Strategy released in 2019 also failed to achieve a more conservative goal of exclusive breastfeeding for 40% of six-month-old babies by 2022.

The repeated failure to improve breastfeeding rates, despite strategies and mounting evidence of the benefits, tells us that no amount of preaching to women about the benefits of breastfeeding will improve breastfeeding rates. As long as time out of the paid workforce comes at such a significant personal cost to women, early cessation of breastfeeding will continue.

If women lack the structural, financial, and cultural support required to breastfeed, they won't be able to do it for as long as is recommended. They will feel individually responsible for a systemic failing, adding further to the stress and pressure of parenthood. A particular sensitivity then arises in response to breastfeeding advocacy where women who weren't able to breastfeed feel personally attacked by efforts to improve breastfeeding rates.

Parents who use formula are understandably distressed by evidence emerging that continues to highlight the health risks of formula use, particularly if they were not made aware of these risks by health professionals. Smith says, "Many women who have been let down by governments refusing to invest in enabling breastfeeding and forced to supplant with formula have every right to be angry. One in three leaves hospital using formula despite 96% starting with breastfeeding."

The 'Fed is Best' movement aimed at inclusion undoubtedly has a debilitating effect on efforts to improve awareness of breastmilk as optimal infant nutrition. In a moment, these three words can erase decades of evidence and absolve policymakers of accountability to better support women in their breastfeeding efforts. Rather than spending time and money to support a mother to breastfeed, we offer her a substandard quick fix and downplay the risks of not breastfeeding. We cannot treat breastfeeding like the health imperative it is unless we are committed to enabling women to pursue it.

ANU also has developed a tool called Mother's Milk that measures the dollar value of human milk produced based on the market value of donor milk. It values my milk production at about $157,892.

Smith hopes breastmilk may be included one day as part of the gross domestic product, estimating the value of milk produced by Australian mothers is about $2bn a year, compared with an annual retail value of formula milk of about $135m.

The new Cost of Not Breastfeeding tool was developed between 2017 and 2019 by Dr Dylan Walters and Alive & Thrive[44], with funding from the Bill & Melinda Gates Foundation. The tool demonstrated that almost 600,000 childhood deaths from diarrhoea and pneumonia each year can be attributed to not breastfeeding, according to global recommendations from WHO and UNICEF[45]. 'It also estimates that 974,956 cases of childhood obesity can be attributed to not breastfeeding according to recommendations each year,' researchers wrote in the *Oxford Journal for Health Policy and Planning*. 'For women, breastfeeding is estimated to have the potential to prevent 98,243 deaths from breast and ovarian cancers as well as type II diabetes each year. This level of avoidable morbidity and mortality translates into global health system treatment costs of US$1.1 billion annually. The economic losses of premature child and women's mortality are estimated to equal US$53.7 billion in future lost earnings each year. The largest component of economic losses, however, is the cognitive losses, which are estimated to equal US$285.4 billion annually.'

Ultimately, if breastmilk has immense value and if this were recognised, it could potentially lead to breastfeeding women being able to earn carbon credits or some form of remuneration that reflected the value of this contribution. These tools bring the value of breastfeeding out of the abstract and put a tangible measure on something that has been considered immeasurable. It also helps women see the real value in their unpaid and often invisible work.

Calculating the total figure of milk I had produced gave me an enormous sense of accomplishment. The blood, sweat, and tears that went into learning how to breastfeed cannot be understated. I cried out of frustration and not knowing why I found it so difficult. My nipples almost fell off at one stage due to poor latching. And all my children were born in the warmer months when nursing a baby was often sweaty work.

The early breastfeeding days were a bit of a blur but I definitely required several lactation consultants, a few late-night calls to the 'help me' hotlines, a trip to the tongue-tie specialist and a few appointments with a psychologist to get through. I had a revolving door of family and friends willing to help, extensive support networks, and the financial means to acquire professional support.

Not everyone has this. Many women talk about the mental distress of breastfeeding as their reason for switching to formula. There will always be instances in which formula use is necessary, but we must accept social responsibility for the lack of support for these women. The blame for this public health and environmental failing cannot rest on individual women.

In Australia, recent changes to the Paid Parental Leave (PPL) scheme have actually reduced some mother's ability to access support in the early-postpartum period. The media coverage surrounding the revamped PPL scheme announced on July 1, 2022, was full of sound bites about the system being more generous and designed to incentivise more men to take more parental leave. It was all about more equally redistributing care responsibility, sharing the disadvantages that come with taking time away from paid work, and breaking down entrenched gender stereotypes.

Women's Economic Equality Taskforce chairwoman Sam Mostyn[46], our current Governor-General, helped design the sweeping reforms and said she was trying to build a more "gender-equal Australia".

Under the new scheme, dads who are partnered to a mother who does not return to paid work between children will no longer be getting PPL. Only fathers partnered to working mothers will be eligible for PPL critical for helping a partner recovering from birth and with care responsibilities.

The hypocrisy of waxing lyrical about needing more dads involved in care work and then withdrawing support in this way is difficult to fathom. It feels like a play to make mothers caring for children in the home feel even more worthless, undervalued, and backward. Not only are they not worthy of support after the birth of a baby, but now their partners are being cut out of leave also.

It makes mothers who choose to remain in a caregiving role feel personally responsible for fewer dads taking less parental leave. Not only is there a huge financial disadvantage for living on one income that makes many parents working in the home feel like a burden, but now those families are also made to feel as if they are letting down the gender-equality movement.

It was a clear withdrawal of support for women in caregiving roles and single-income families. One of the stranger parts about the new scheme was the silence and lack of transparency with which these changes were made. Initially, people didn't understand the trade-off the new system was making, and once they became aware they were too disoriented and disenfranchised to speak up. Not a single story has been aired in the media about this gross withdrawal of support for working dads.

Sarah Rotham (not her real name) contacted the ABC, her federal member Ian Goodenough, and Social Services Minister Amanda Rishworth. A staff member from Rishworth's office responded to inform them that, indeed, the PPL scheme was now available only to working families. "Our family is a working family, despite being a single-income family," Rotham told me in an interview I did for *The Weekend Australian*. "Their new system is not pro-dads or pro-women. Why is a Dad's access to paid leave only granted on the basis that the birth mother has been working enough? Why does she need to earn his entitlement? They acknowledge women need to recover after childbirth, but only if they've been working. If they're a stay-at-home mother, then they do not need that support for recovery apparently. We feel so let down by the government. This is not a step forward for society."

Not only was the announcement disingenuous about the withdrawal of support, and a raw deal for many families, but it was also trumpeted as an expansion of leave when it demonstrably was not. At the time of the 'extension', the primary caregiver could still access only 18 weeks' paid parental leave, which they have been able to do since the Fairer Paid Parental Leave Bill in 2015. There was still an additional two weeks reserved for the other parent, it was just no longer called dad and partner pay. This pattern will continue and, as the projected increases occur, so does the reserved component. Even when the PPL scheme reaches 26 weeks in 2026, the primary carer will still be able to access only a maximum of 22 weeks. What has been sold as an increase of eight weeks is, for a parent who wishes to take maximum leave, actually only half that. Still an increase, but with a huge catch. It was made out to be something it wasn't.

The only difference now is that mothers are free to take less paid leave if they choose and return to work while still bleeding from a wound the size of a dinner plate on their uterus. PPL for both parents most certainly is a large part of the solution to gender equality, but the policy we ended up with and which was pitched as more progressive, requires women to sacrifice their own much-needed leave to increase dads' leave. It wasn't just the Women's Economic Equality Taskforce driving these changes. Both sides of government and a large group of childcare and parenthood advocate bodies also supported the changes. Why do they do this?

I believe many in power genuinely, but mistakenly, believe the only solution to advancing gender equality is minimising both parents' involvement in care. If progress is to be made in postpartum support, we cannot continue to impose blanket policy on men and women aimed at achieving completely arbitrary divisions of labour with complete disregard for the unique physiological experience of mothers. The antenatal and postpartum period shapes the parents we become and determines outcomes for children. It is here we must focus our policy and cultural efforts, in laying strong foundations for parents and babies, if we are to change for the better.

CHAPTER SEVEN

An Extra Set of Hands

When my son was born, I could not understand why it was so hard. I couldn't work out why a sense of dread crept up into my chest when my husband left the house in the morning to go to work. I didn't realise that in the history of humans prior to the 20th century, the care of a baby was basically never tasked to one person for extended periods of time during the day. That's a modern invention that isn't working out. Mothers in some hunter-gatherer tribes that still exist today hold their own baby for as little as 25% of the time during the day in the early months[47]. As we discussed in the previous chapter, evidence exists that throughout history, and still in many Eastern cultures today, mothers were afforded many weeks of rest, lying down and with round-the-clock care in the postpartum period[48].

I spent my early months and years of motherhood thinking I was the problem, that I simply wasn't really cut out for it. There was reluctance in asking for help because I felt like I was imposing on people to assist me with a role I should have been able to do myself. Rather than making a reasonable request for help, I felt stupid and incapable. Instead of asking what is wrong with our mothers, we need to start looking at the environment they are working within. We need to ask why we have remained wilfully ignorant and even enabled the continued erosion of support systems for mothers.

It's clear to anyone who has ever been a mother that it's not a one-woman job. The phrase 'it takes a village' takes on a whole new meaning when children arrive. Anthropological research confirms we weren't meant to do this alone – that a single person simply cannot sustain the level of emotional and physical labour required to meet such an intensive and high-dependency period. Yet the sole primary caregiver myth and expectations persist.

Rather than cultural and policy shifts that actually supported a mother to give care or rebuilt community around her, we began profiting off parental stress and isolation. Industrialisation and endless economic growth gradually drew most people into the workplace, stripped back the social fabric of communities, and then started selling parents solutions to their newfound isolation.

The appearance of door-to-door salesmen and even, to an extent, handymen, represented a kind of economic growth that directly responded to isolated caregivers at home. Many of the products that emerged here were genuine time and manual-labour savers like vacuum cleaners, but over time the economic growth in this area became exploitative and predatory. Mothers in the home were often alone, in need of help, and perhaps more vulnerable to marketing. We sold them make-up and skincare door-to-door.

Over time, we have invented more and more baby accessories and 'sets of hands' with the promise that if they just buy this next new gadget or product, things would be easier. The baby market exploded with bouncers, high-chairs, dummies, bottles, capsules, rockers, and play pens in attempts to compensate for this lack of help. We sold women answer after answer to their problems, and this continues today. We put mothers in a problematic situation and then, instead of addressing the root cause, we sold them poor substitutes for a village.

Not only did women entering the workplace boost economies and GDPs around the world through their earnings, but the void they left in the care sector was also voraciously monetised. We address the commodification of early childhoods in detail in a future chapter that looks at early education and care, but at its core the advent of daycare was another 'pair of hands' that was sold to families who were increasingly reliant on dual incomes. This formed a major part of the global economic growth which resulted from women entering paid work.

This process of economic growth was considered vital and somewhat overdue, as the single-income economy was beginning to show signs of reaching its limits and worrying predictions were emerging about the potential for economic collapse in the future. In 1972, the influential work of 17 researchers was compiled and published in a controversial book called *The Limits to Growth*[49]. The book warned that if the current trajectory of resource depletion, population growth, and industrialisation remained unchanged it would result in extreme resource scarcity, widespread productivity decline, industry slowdown, and uncontrollable population collapse.

The claims were heavily criticised as alarmist and ridiculed when some of the predictions failed to eventuate. However, it was republished in 2004, then in 2012, theoretical chemist and Nobel Peace Prize winner John Scales Avery said, "Although specific predictions in resource availability in *Limits to Growth* lacked accuracy, its basic thesis—that unlimited economic growth on a finite planet is impossible—was indisputably correct."

It's likely that technological innovation and efficiencies may have muted some of the predictions made in the book, but the workforce powering the economy also changed markedly in the 50 years since the book's publication. Women boosted economies and productivity in ways that would have been difficult to predict in the 1970s, essentially propping up economies in the early stages of decline and masking underlying symptoms of failing economies. However, there is also a limit to finding new populations to boost economic growth.

Consider a hypothetical scenario where we somehow enable all mothers to work full-time from birth and enjoy the economic growth that results – what then? Do we explore legalising child labour as the next major shot in the arm for global economies? Do we send the elderly back to work? Obviously, I'm being sarcastic here, but in all seriousness we have to acknowledge that increasing workforce participation simply buys us time to solve the larger problem of global systems that have come to rely on growth economies – it is not a solution in itself. Did we use the boom time of women entering the workforce to set ourselves up for a sustainable future full of equitable opportunity and quality living standards for all? No. We used this to justify the merit of existing systems and tell ourselves a nice bedtime story that capitalism in its current form could indeed ensure the future of humankind.

The development of long daycare, as we know it, was fundamental to supporting women's extraordinary foray into paid work. Though many would not have recognised this at the time, countries that did not invest public funds in daycares and early education were irrevocably set down a path of commodifying as much childcare as possible. Most countries opened the doors to private equity to service this demand for childcare, and for-profit childcare businesses took over. At a similar time, Nordic regions and countries governed by socialist rather than individualist principles set about building public childcare systems, in the long term achieving very different solutions to early education and care which is largely not a profit-making exercise in those countries.

With the informal care economy rapidly displaced by the formal care economy, what remained of our time with our children and loved ones was time-pressured and exhausting. Once again, this opened new opportunities for market growth outside of the childcare industry.

We began selling parents solutions for lack of sleep and time.

Privately-run sleep schools, robotic rockers or cribs, and eventually drugs like melatonin. To compensate for lack of support, we sold mothers solutions that reduced a child's dependence on caregivers, arguably before they were developmentally ready. Daycare has spawned a whole market of accessories – special sleeping bags for children to nap in at daycare and labelling systems marketed to parents years earlier than the usual school-age need for labelling clothes.

Sleep training rose to popularity in response to an obvious need to not be sleep deprived while carrying out the task of raising children without a village and possibly also while engaging in paid work. Trying to override the natural circadian rhythms of babies is actually quite a normal response to what is an unmanageable situation for many families. The administration of paracetamol and antibiotics in babies and children is commonplace and has skyrocketed in the last 30 years because parents are stressed and desperate to be able to use care. Paracetamol has become a way of coping with a sick child in busy daily life, yet research does not support perceptions that paracetamol is normally a necessary or beneficial treatment of fevers[50].

By the time Australian children reach 12 years of age, 95% will have been administered paracetamol[51]. Compare this to Australian Bureau of Statistics survey findings that liquid-form paracetamol was present in only 62% of households with a child under five in 1992, and we have a clear generational shift.

In Australia today, paracetamol is administered largely indiscriminately to children in both clinical and home settings despite an incomplete understanding of how the molecule works. We know it inhibits pain receptors called prostaglandins and chemical messengers that regulate the body temperature, but the how—the exact mechanism of how it does this—continues to elude scientists. Adults and children also metabolise paracetamol differently, so while we have enormous data sets on widespread adult use over many decades, the extremely widespread use in children is a more recent development and a lot remains to be seen in longitudinal research cohorts consisting of babies and children. Better understanding of long-term impacts will take time.

Geelong-based paediatrician Peter Hewson points to both lack of benefit and potential harm of routine paracetamol use in the treatment of childhood fever. In his paper for an independent medical review journal, *Australian Prescriber*, he points to evidence showing paracetamol can inhibit the natural immune response and prolong the amount of time a person sheds a virus. He also argues that research has been unable to establish that paracetamol is effective in preventing febrile seizures or improving a child's appetite or fluid intake. "Treat the child, not the thermometer," he argues. "It has previously been mistakenly accepted that all febrile children with infective illness require medication. We need to question this phenomenon as another example of society's reliance on drugs ... Parents and doctors understandably need to feel they have something to offer sick, miserable children. However, cuddles, comfort and fluids are likely to be a safer and healthier alternative to drugs."

It's pretty clear that our increasing use of pain medication is as much about our lifestyle and work patterns as it is about the kids. The use of pain relief to keep up with increasingly busy family lives is well documented in research and anecdotally. It's the great enabler of our jam-packed schedules and fast-paced lifestyles. It can buy us a few hours at work before the daycare centre calls to tell us our child has a temperature, it can help us 'push through' an illness when really our body needs to rest. Kids raised on routine use of paracetamol may likely grow into adults who self-medicate rather than taking a break. Work schedules and financial demands may not permit rest in many instances, but strong cultural emphasis on 'busyness' and productivity also makes it harder to slow down even if given the option.

At the height of the COVID-19 outbreak, Australians were buying about 65 million packets of paracetamol annually. We have experienced nationwide shortages of Children's Panadol at least once a year since 2020. We just can't get enough. Percentage increases in year-on-year sales growth of Panadol frequently enter the double digits in the Australian market. Yet another extremely lucrative market emerges from the work and care predicament.

The increasing use of paracetamol has led to ever increasing overdoses. While young children make up a small number of overall paracetamol overdose cases in Australia, in 2019 the University of Sydney reported a staggering increase of 44% in hospitalisations from 2007 to 2017. Figures like this prompted the Therapeutic Goods Administration (TGA) to rule in favour of reducing the packet size of paracetamol tablets for sale in non-pharmacy outlets.

Aside from the health risks associated with overuse of paracetamol in children, equally concerning is the way our increasing reliance on pain medication can inform a child's future relationship with pain and medication. We are modelling 'pill popping' as the solution rather than addressing root causes of constant illness or pain though lifestyle changes or non-pharmaceutical treatments. We are sabotaging the development of psychological skills involved in managing discomfort.

Managing pain and discomfort will continue to be critical to healthcare and recovery, a hallmark of modern society, but in a counterintuitive sense practising restraint can improve our ability to do this. More is not necessarily better when it comes to managing pain. Studies are now linking increased use of analgesia with increased pain sensitivity. In 2017, Norwegian scientists showed this increased pain sensitivity created a vicious cycle and predicted future persistent use of pain medication in a sample of more than 10,000 adults.

The more we rely on medicine to make the pain go away, the less able we are to tolerate mild, temporary discomfort.

As well as childhood medications, quick fixes for childhood nutrition became a lucrative business. The markets for processed baby food and processed food in general exploded to save parents from labour-intensive and time-consuming food preparation and give them more 'quality time' with their children. The consequences of this dramatic change in diet have been serious and widespread, with obesity levels and chronic nutrition-related health problems skyrocketing. In 2024, research from the George Institute for Global health found 78% of baby food companies studied were failing to comply with WHO salt and sugar requirements. All were falsely labelling food and making misleading claims.

Rather than policies that protect and support breastfeeding or a parent's ability to prepare food, governments have time and again sanctioned this health compromise. We have traded our health for money. In the context of women entering paid work, policies such as Paid Parental Leave and public health campaigns were ignored while incentives to enter paid work were dialled up. As a result, infant nutrition was turned into a multi-billion dollar enterprise. Formula companies went from niche markets for tiny babies to global entities selling milk products for children up to preschool age. Where they once had to use predatory and misleading tactics to establish themselves in a market, such as claiming scientific 'formula' was superior to breastmilk, formula companies were handed a captive market made up of mothers entering the paid workforce. People had no choice but to use formula.

Formula companies even gave out free samples door-to-door in disadvantaged communities across the global south. Nestlé boycotts in response to these tactics is well documented. The main cause for protest is marketing tactics used in vulnerable populations and the promotion of infant formula by use of free samples thereby interfering with breastmilk supply enough to create long-term dependence on formula.

Formula companies also expanded by establishing themselves as a solution not just for mothers lacking support but also tired and time-poor parents battling fussy eaters. Their products are aggressively marketed well into toddlerhood and age ranges where formula milk is no longer a nutritional requirement, preying on insecurities around toddlers getting adequate nutrition. A 2022 WHO report found infant formula companies were targeting expectant and new mothers on social media platforms and tailoring advertising to them that was often hard to identify as paid ads.

'Fewer than half of babies worldwide are breastfed per WHO recommendations, resulting in economic losses of nearly $350 billion each year,' according to the medical journal[52]. 'Meanwhile, the industry rakes in around $55 billion each year and spends about $3 billion on marketing—despite an international code adopted by the WHO's decision-making body in 1981 that prohibits the marketing of such formulas in the majority of instances'[53].

Even night nannies, postpartum doulas, and breastfeeding and weaning courses are also benign but still clear examples of the market economy responding to the erosion of the village. These coping mechanisms have been introduced gradually and almost imperceptibly over many years. These have all arisen out of necessity, but often they perpetuate the problem and don't adequately meet the needs of parents and children. This has bred another set of problems.

Talking about how deeply flawed our approach to childhood and parenthood has become may feel depressing but this is a necessary process on the road to recovery. If we don't recognise how the devaluation of caregiving is being driven by commerce, if we don't understand how far reaching and insidious the problems are, we can't hope to address them. This is a bad situation, but it's not beyond help.

CHAPTER EIGHT

Giving Parents Time to Parent

In an economy that now often demands dual incomes, perhaps the most difficult problem to solve is how to actually give parents time to parent. It's all well and good to list the reasons care work should be valued and why it is vital to our wellbeing but what's the point of this exercise if it's something we can never realistically have? When there is so much money to be made in the short term through incomes generated by parents in paid work and through the additional markets created due to their time scarcity, giving parents time can seem like an unaffordable cost to society and to individuals.

The truth is, we have dug ourselves into a financial and health hole. We now have a dangerous dependency on ever-increasing incomes and work hours. It will take vast resources and ingenuity to disentangle ourselves from the new normal we find ourselves in. We will have to go through a period of struggle and strain to return to a sustainable balance of life and work. The economies that supply resources to meet the most basic human needs like food and medicine, rely on year-on-year growth. Growth has become a built-in feature. Dual incomes are a built-in feature. Like junkies, we are now individually and collectively dependent on growth and will do almost anything to get it, regardless of the long-term consequences. So, convincing people that change to our care and work systems is urgently needed is a tall order.

As responsible citizens we must train ourselves to frequently step out of the short-term-need mindset. What are the long-term consequences of this choice? Is this the kind of society I want for future generations? Is this what I value? We must build the muscles of reminding ourselves why we are changing even though it can be difficult. We must remind ourselves daily that the cost of doing nothing is far greater than the cost of giving parents time with their children. The only reason we have gotten by in this system for so long is because women have compensated. Women continue to silently sacrifice their own health and incomes to carry out care work in unsupported conditions. We carry on over-functioning because if we don't, the first people we hurt are our children. Our over-functioning partially shields our children from what we can see is a terrible trade-off.

Like most mothers I know, I'm operating at the upper limits of human functioning – pregnant for three of the last seven years, breastfeeding for six, sleep deprived to the point that it's a state of being. Psychoanalysing children, picking up more paid work, trying to be fun, and constantly duelling with the pile of laundry[54].

We are learning there is a point at which working more becomes less productive; that there is a limit to human capital. We steadily deplete the informal care economy that underpins the market economy and wonder why productivity is stagnating and birth rates are falling. We have to decide how much of our time to care for each other and ourselves is worth protecting and, conversely, how much paid work and economic growth is enough? What is sustainable?

Growth economies are exhausting reserves of endurance, benevolence, and goodwill among the people who have typically provided unpaid care from which profits are made. It is time for the government and the private sector to start seriously reinvesting in the unpaid care they rely on.

Carer credit schemes, a practice where primary carers earn money towards their retirement while in a caregiving role, are in place in wealthy, socially-progressive nations such as Sweden and Germany but have repeatedly failed to gain traction in Australian politics. The Australian Human Rights Commission has been recommending the implementation of a carer credits scheme since 2011, and in 2023 the Select Committee on Work and Care also recommended carer credits following their inquiry into better balancing work and care responsibilities. Carer credits are accumulated well beyond the paid parental leave period, during which superannuation should also be paid.

Not only do carer credits present an opportunity to achieve a fairer society, close the superannuation gender gap in Australia and better support unpaid carers, there is also a strong economic case for this practice. In 2021, global financial consultancy firm, Mercer, modelled a superannuation contribution for Australian carers after the firm's global pension index revealed many other countries contributed to social security for unpaid caregivers. Senior partner, Dr David Knox, said an investment in superannuation equated to a saving on future aged-pension spending. "This is a way of making sure that people who take time out of the workforce to care for young children or ageing parents, predominantly women, have a more dignified retirement than they would otherwise have."

Knox said falling birth rates would only increase the pressure on governments to better support unpaid contributions in the future. "Superannuation is paid on annual leave, it's paid on long service leave, it should also be paid on parental leave as this is an extension of that," he explains. "Yes, it is a government expenditure, but we're supporting those who are caring for young children and having young children means you're supporting the next generation of taxpayers in the society and that's what we need. We're an ageing population and the Australian birth rate is well below what we call replacement rate."

The unwillingness to contribute to a caregiver's pension is emblematic of a wider issue where the reluctance to support the unpaid care economy is not for lack of sound policies to implement, but a lack of public support and political will. It's one thing to design policies that resource the unpaid care economy, it's another thing entirely to convince people that this sector is worth resourcing. That the unpaid contribution is just as vital as the paid. That a woman's time is as valuable as any man's.

The struggle to value and retain the natural environment has experienced similar publicity issues in that people expect natural capital to be free at the same time as exploiting it. The carbon credits scheme introduced under the Gillard government in 2011, though not without its issues, succeeded in bringing nature's value out of the abstract and into the marketplace. It ultimately allowed many landholders to access a form of compensation for retaining biodiversity and natural capital rather than personally shouldering the opportunity cost of leaving vegetation in the ground. The idea of earning 'credits' in exchange for cultivating a rather intangible but extremely valuable resource seems to be slightly more palatable than direct subsidies.

Natural capital conservation is now recognised by banks in Australia. In 2020, I reported on the increasingly common practice of banks cutting interest rates where landholders could demonstrate conservation practices[55]. This concept could also be applied to human capital, with carers who are actively building human capital and reducing the burden on the public health system, recognised by discounted health insurance. Parents are stewards of human capital in the same way farmers are stewards of the natural capital we rely on for survival.

Australian National University Honorary Professor Julie Smith has sought to encourage investment in the unpaid care sector by creating algorithms that enable governments to measure carbon emissions avoided by breastfeeding (mentioned in Chapter 5). Professor Smith's 'Green Feeding Tool' is designed to help governments justify policies that facilitate extended breastfeeding, like better paid parental leave, as contributing to long-term emissions reductions. Professor Smith has also extensively modelled the public health cost savings of improving breastfeeding rates. She's not reinventing the policy but finding new ways to demonstrate and measure the value of said policy in a tangible sense.

Professor Smith is also an economic historian and has dedicated much of her professional life to developing innovative ways to resource the unpaid care economy. "We're in this time in history where we haven't worked out how we're going to sustain our workforce, we've reached the limit, it's crunch time for our care economy," she says. "We have very gendered and blinkered ideologies driving policies that don't see unpaid work as work. We have to reframe supports as investments in the unpaid economy. It's the underpinnings of the market because it's producing your labour force so why wouldn't you invest in it?"

Senator Barbara Pocock, in her previous work as a Professor of Economics, also explored the way affording families more time to care could reduce carbon emissions. 'Time poor workers and households will place convenience above a reduced carbon footprint when they are pressed,' she writes in her 2012 book, *Time Bomb*. 'They will try to buy quick solutions when their commute eats into their time or when their job crowds out time for changing their habits.' She argues that the impact of increased paid work on the capacity to reduce waste, consumption, and energy use warrants further examination.

We often clearly state the problem and, as we demonstrate

in this book, there are many and varied solutions that could be implemented. Ultimately, whether we resource the unpaid care sector in the future isn't about whether it is possible or whether we understand the problem properly, it will depend on our ability to see the value in that contribution in the context of both climate and human health. It will depend on our ability to significantly shift existing world views and value systems.

Social philosopher Anne Manne envisions a new paradigm where society values unpaid contributions such as care and volunteering as equally important as paid contributions. "It needs to be a radical shift where we really re-evaluate what it is we value in our lives." Manne doesn't identify as a Christian but appeared on the Centre for Public Christianity's podcast earlier this year. "We don't have enough of a sense of honour in care work, there's an intricacy and an intimacy about giving care, a reading of another person where they are at that moment. It's like emotional braille, feeling your way to where they are and a kind of alchemy if you respond to them in the right way. It's certainly true of a child but it's true of someone with dementia as well."

Manne argues extensively for policies that directly remunerate unpaid care work in real time. She flips the narrative of carers as welfare bludgers and instead identifies people who benefit from care responsibilities but don't perform that work themselves as 'care bludgers'. "If I may borrow from the likes of Joe Hockey and join in the long tradition of rhetoric around welfare bludgers, well what about care bludgers? If people avoid care responsibilities the implications for others are enormous," she explained.

Most people like the idea of care, they like the idea of 'wellbeing', 'mothers' and 'family' and 'freedom of choice' and 'equality', but are we willing to pay for these things? Assigning true value to care work will seem expensive in the short term because we are accustomed to women providing that work for free and at their personal disadvantage. Our economy and life as we know it has relied on the exploitation of unpaid carers for so long that resistance is inevitable – we simply lack the imagination to see any other way.

If the care contribution continues to come with significant financial and professional penalty, families will be increasingly unable to provide this contribution and without policies that resource unpaid care, caring will slowly but surely be outsourced to the market at both ends of life. As American author Robert Kuttner writes[56], 'When everything is for sale, the person who volunteers time, who helps a stranger, who agrees to work for a modest wage out of commitment to the public good... who forgoes the opportunity to free ride, begins to feel like a sucker.' It will require creativity, as well as bravery to bridge political divides and properly investigate ways to retain the kind of care that money can't buy.

Another factor actively preventing the implementation or even just the investigation of solutions which would give parents time to care, is politics. So often in this space politics gets in the way of good policy. Both sides of politics are uncomfortable with the idea that many women have no choice but to return to paid work just months after their baby is born.

Then Shadow Minister for Women, Sussan Ley, told the House of Representatives in 2023, "While improvements in economic participation are welcomed, if they are attributed to women having no other choice than to go back to work to make ends meet then this is concerning." Ley's comments foreshadow a subtle departure from a brand of gender equality that is entirely contingent on a woman's presence in the workplace.

Self-described social progressive and former Independent Member for Goldstein, Zoe Daniels, also recognises that equality means more than rushing women back to work. "It also includes better supporting women who want to take time out of the workforce when they have young children so they don't take a giant leap backwards which they can never bridge," she told *The Australian*, citing paid parental leave extensions and superannuation contributions while on leave as top of her agenda.

In 2023, the Labor government made some clear moves towards improving social supports for parents. It introduced a significant extension of the Single Parenting Payment by raising the cut-off age from eight to 14 years. It was a clear reversal of the Gillard Government's 2008 decision to wind back single parenting payments to force more single mothers to replace caregiving responsibilities with the 'dignity of work'. The Gillard government clearly equated the work of caring for a child with unemployment, while the recent extension signals a long overdue shift toward valuing the role of a consistent primary caregiver in a child's life.

The abolition of the ParentsNext scheme also indicates a move away from transactional 'work for welfare'-style payments for parents which fail to take into account the unpaid labour already involved in the care of children. ParentsNext issued payments for disadvantaged parents of children from nine months to six years old, which were conditional upon harsh compliance requirements such as participation in work experience and upskilling courses. An inquiry in 2024 found the program amounted to coercive control.

The government also responded to the Women's Economic Equality Taskforce's calls to increase the rate of Commonwealth Rental Assistance with a 15% rise to improve housing security for women and families experiencing financial distress often due to time engaged in unpaid caregiving. 'Australian women have told us, as they have told you, that they are tired of being the heartbeat of the Australian economy providing the essential infrastructure that is care, but with little reward or valuing for doing so,' the taskforce wrote to the Federal Minister for Women Katy Gallagher ahead of the May 2023 Budget. 'Women are tired of waiting for the right time to be prioritised.'

More recently, the new leader of the Greens Party, Larissa Waters, also spoke out about the importance of supporting care work. "It's time parents are rewarded, not penalised, for dedicating themselves to the precious first year of a baby's life," she said. "Twenty-six weeks at minimum wage is not enough. Families are being forced to make decisions that keep the bills paid rather than being supported to choose what's right for them and their kids. Hard working new parents are sacrificing precious time with their family, while big corporations make record profits and one in three of them pay no tax."

Apart from these lucid moments, politics around women, mothers, and children usually erupts into nonsensical name-calling or turns immediately to childcare. Realistic policies that assign value to the care contributions already exist and are in place in countries widely considered socially progressive, but they haven't been able to garner political consensus in Australia. The practice of allowing families to split their income equally between both parents to lower the tax threshold can ease financial strain in single-income families or those where one parent works part-time. The policy was introduced in Canada in recent years but when income splitting was raised by Liberal Senator Matt Canavan in 2021 it was widely condemned as a way of 'keeping mothers at home' rather than a mechanism to ease the financial strain that comes with caregiving.

It is curious that resistance to policies that serve to improve conditions for unpaid caregivers—a traditionally oppressed and marginalised group—comes mostly from 'progressive' and left-leaning quarters. Left-leaning politicians seem determined to improve conditions for caregivers only by enabling them to avoid care work rather than changing the factors that make care contributions so disadvantageous to the individual.

Even more curious is the willingness of conservatives to engage in socialist strategies, policies that translate to increased spending on social supports, in order to conserve traditional 'family values'.

Nonetheless, childcare subsidies continue to represent one of the single largest government expenditures to support Australian families. Reports of childcare providers absorbing increases in the subsidies and avoiding high-needs children who require more time and resources is to be expected in a sector that has largely been allowed to become a profit-making exercise. It should come as no surprise that taxpayer dollars end up beefing up profit margins rather than finding their intended target of financially distressed families in need of support.

The benefits of the childcare subsidy as it stands also fall spectacularly unevenly across women from different socioeconomic and geographic groups – much to the frustration of State Member for Euroa and mother of two, Annabelle Cleeland. Cleeland lobbies constantly for improved supports for regional families in her rural Victorian communities. "Our current childcare system is a model where you need to fit in—both geographically and logistically—or be left out," she says. "We are at a crossroads where governments need to reimagine how we deliver childcare and early-learning education."

If childcare is to become truly universal in a country with a landmass the size of Australia, subsidies must extend to alternative models of care more readily available in regional areas such as private help or parent care. Increased investment in education programs to allow parents to deliver educational and supportive early experiences will be vital. Publicly funded universal childcare is all well and good in a country the size of Tasmania with a high population density and world leading public transport systems, but the reality of universality of any service in Australia will always be a vastly different and complex beast.

The future of policies that actually give parents time rests on a few central questions – do we want families to have the choice to provide the care of their own children or should placing babies and young children in institutional care remain the only supported model of care? Is caregiving a luxury or a basic human right? Is a stay-at-home parent in a child's earliest years a disposable social function or something that must be supported for the wellbeing of wider society?

Historically, the cost of care was built into the single-income wage, which was supplemented by the 'breadwinner' component added to the minimum wage of men who were providing for families. This ensured families were effectively remunerated for the care contribution and in this sense, unpaid care work had more currency in 1950 than it does today. Rather than retaining an additional wage component for families who remained on a single income, the breadwinner component was completely abolished shortly after equal pay was legislated in 1953. Regardless of a breadwinner's gender, if they are providing for a family on a single income do they not require similar supplementation now as was built into the wage in 1950?

On this issue, socially conservative and socially progressive political parties must examine the common goal of facilitating freedom of choice for women. If both ends of the political spectrum could stop disagreeing for the sake of argument, support measures for unpaid care contributions could close gender pay gaps faster than any childcare subsidy. Social progressives have to decide how much it is appropriate to dictate to women what decisions are in their best interests. Social conservatives have to decide how much family values are worth in dollars, if they willing to put their money where their mouth is.

CHAPTER NINE

Welcome to the World of Daycare Research

I discuss research findings in this book not to be accusatory or to make people feel bad about themselves, but because I believe we must consider the evidence base as we go about building optimal family support and care systems. The evidence base has a long history of being politicised, avoided, and ignored to suit political or ideological agendas. It is vital that policy, parenting, and early-childhood practices are informed by the evidence base, not simply opinions and ideology. Research isn't the whole picture, it is not immune to politics, market forces, and personal bias, but it's a very important place to start.

When research findings challenge our beliefs or our practices, we often feel uncomfortable. If we interrogate this discomfort we might find we can dismiss the findings or that it presents an opportunity for positive change. Policy cannot be guided by the convenient option, the option that doesn't hurt people's feelings, the cheapest option or doing 'what we've always done'. We can't justify policy because 'everyone is doing it' or because it's the option we want to be right because it aligns with our views and beliefs.

Also, the research findings I discuss in this book highlight systemic issues rather than personal failings. Whenever research is raised that causes parents to feel guilty or lash out with anger, this happens because they are often taking personal responsibility for a systemic failing. We aren't criticising parents, we are criticising the systems they are being forced to operate within. Living in individualised cultures such as those evident in Westernised countries has conditioned us to take personal responsibility for problems well beyond our scope of influence. This chapter can make for uncomfortable reading but being aware that we are part of a system that has not had our best interests as a priority, helps to lessen the blow.

While we may be parenting within systems that often leave us with little choice around how we raise our children, sometimes there is still room for small changes that can make a big difference to our quality of life. There may or may not be opportunities to generate change from an individual level or bottom-up approach. There may be moments or seasons where we are feeling supported and do have the capacity to make changes at an individual level. This is when having access to transparent information is vital – we can't do better if we don't know better.

As an example, an important reason I know my phone use is problematic is because I have access to research findings around the negative effects of screen time. I might have had a deeper, intuitive sense that staring at a screen all day is probably not ideal, but the research is the wake-up call and confirmation I needed to change. The articles are tough reading. I feel a wave of regret and guilt and shame but because I know better, I can aim to reduce phone use.

I could push down the feelings of discomfort by trying to undermine the research or criticise the research methods. I could also demonise those who carried out the research by arguing they are being disrespectful or mean to people who have screen addictions. Even justify my excessive screen use by saying I need it for work or to stay in touch with friends, but I know deep down that my phone use is problematic and therefore I make ongoing attempts to develop healthier habits.

In another sense, the disconnectedness of community, the isolation and lack of support many parents feel also makes us more vulnerable to screen addictions. We rely more heavily on our screens to connect with others. Our screen reliance has partly systemic causes, especially if we lack access to psychological support, use it to numb financial stressors or if we want to zone out from overwhelming care responsibilities. Again, this isn't about pointing the finger at mothers – phone use is largely a symptom of broader problems.

Another example could be research around the negative health effects of processed meats. An under-supported parent might be relying on chicken nuggets or sausage sandwich dinners just to get through the day or because it's more affordable. Then they finally collapse on the couch after the kids go to bed only to find a news article pop up on their phone about the dangers of processed meats. This is going to be uncomfortable for a parent who feels like they don't have the capacity for change, but it doesn't mean we shouldn't still be aware of the health impacts of processed meats.

Food processing companies and governments and public health departments have a responsibility to make sure legislation and policies are in place that ensure fresh, healthy food is available to all. Research findings enable us to hold the powers that be accountable. We could just ignore the research because we don't want struggling parents to feel bad, but in the long run this is actually doing them a disservice.

Awareness and transparency means governments have a public health obligation to mount campaigns and introduce policies that can help families improve their health and wellbeing. Having access to accurate information also means that on an individual level a person may one day find themselves with agency and can then make dietary changes. Not being transparent around early-childhood evidence leaves parents flying blind and relying on anecdotes but it also allows governments to remain unaccountable for policies that aren't supported by the evidence base or aren't in the best interests of family health.

Finally, doing the right thing is almost never the easiest or cheapest option. Sometimes, the most important changes are the most difficult. If we refuse to acknowledge research, we are doing ourselves and future generations a huge disservice. Regardless of what we can do on a personal level, these discussions are necessary to inform the top-down approaches that can help us eventually, if not right now.

If childcare settings are to be endorsed as an effective substitute for family and community support that many of us no longer have, we must have proof that it supports child development and parental wellbeing.

In this book I use the term 'daycare' to mean childcare delivered for children under three. I use the term 'preschool' to mean childcare delivered for children over three. I oppose the use of umbrella terms like Early Childhood Education and Care (ECEC), because they fail to distinguish the crucially different roles of early-learning settings at different ages and development stages. Daycare is not the same as preschool, and to equate one with the other undermines the quality of both.

It is vital and logical that we use language that reflects the neurological and developmental differences of a nine-month-old baby and a four-year-old child. Without these distinctions, we risk misappropriating findings related to older children onto infants – a common and damaging misrepresentation of the evidence base. Different behaviours and teaching strategies are required of educators in daycare and preschool settings. What works in supporting development of preschool-aged children is not effective—or even detrimental—at younger ages.

I challenge the use of the term 'educators' as opposed to 'childcare workers'. This reinforces the idea that 'caring as work' is somehow less important or less respected and distinct from 'educating'. Acts of care in our early years represent our most fundamental education and learning of the world around us. Through the care we receive, we learn if people are to be trusted, how to interact with people, cooperation, reciprocation, communication and more. Care and education are one and the same thing, particularly in the first 1000 days of a child's life. Emotional regulation, the ability to focus on a task, working memory, and a strong sense of self and belonging – these are essential characteristics of effective learners later on. These characteristics can only be learned in care environments and relationships that foster security and lower stress levels. They are not skills that can be rote learned through direct instruction or written up on a chalkboard, they are care experiences that we internalise.

As we discussed in Chapter 1, an infant in chronically stressful situations learns that the world is a stressful place. In technical terms, when the hypothalamic-pituitary-adrenal (HPA) axis is activated for prolonged periods in infancy, it can mature to be permanently off-balance and circulate sustained elevated levels of stress hormones even in the absence of threats. Researchers have proposed this occurs because HPA hormones, while triggering the stress response, also trigger growth of the glands within the axis. This was an advantage in an evolutionary sense, because babies raised in dangerous environments were more likely to survive as adults with a heightened and sensitive response to threats.

For a baby or child in modern environments who develops this brain chemistry, it quickly becomes maladaptive because they will find themselves in physically safe environments in which heightened response to potential dangers is often disadvantageous. This brain chemistry, developing enlarged glands to secrete stress hormones, is extremely difficult and many argue impossible to undo.

It may be reduced through consistent and repeated experiences of safe environments and relationships, but it can't be 'taught' in a classroom sense.

The people who assume the crucial role of caring for us and largely determining the emotional wiring we will live with, certainly require a title that reflects the importance and gravity of their work, but why does this necessitate removing the term 'care' from the job title? It's telling that daycare advocates felt it necessary to remove the words 'care and work' from a title in order for the job to be better valued. This is an obvious manifestation of internalised belief systems where education is valued but care work is not.

Convincing ourselves that childcare workers are doing the same job as primary school teachers isn't actually addressing the devaluation and root cause of the problem driving poor work conditions and poor quality care, it's manipulating our current values to apply to daycare centres. We value high grades, high-status jobs, and material and professional success. So, if we align daycare with the school system, direct instruction and formal education, we are tricking people into valuing early-life carers by creating the illusion that we are raising a generation of baby Einsteins.

We see direct evidence of this attempt to align with the formal education system in the rising trend of graduation days in daycare centres and preschools. It's a constant centring of the 'education' over the care. Phrases like 'we're not just wiping bums all day' suggest that keeping babies comfortable is somehow not as valuable as teaching them colours or moon phases. It's this idea that daycare is only acceptable or valuable if it is an academic exercise with measurable outcomes like reports, milestones, and graduations rather than fundamental to our emotion regulation and wellbeing. Soft skills that are harder to measure and brag about, even more difficult to verify and project out to the world. Imagine an Instagram post about how good at regulating their emotions your child is.

In using language that values childcare workers appropriately, we hope to shift attitudes to better value paid care work, and over time this could lead to better pay and working conditions. Better conditions for childcare workers means better outcomes for thousands of Australian children who will continue to use childcare each day for reasons outside their control. It's more effective as a long-term solution to educate people about the value of care and the long-term implications rather than calling it something it isn't.

Daycare and preschool are not school and the terms should not be used interchangeably. We risk losing the distinction that daycare and preschool have a very different function to formal schooling, which typically begins at age five. Formal, full-time education is not necessary or effective for children under five, yet when we use language such as 'going to school' for two year olds, we introduce the expectation that education in formal settings *is* necessary for toddlers and preschoolers. Is this language used to reassure parents that daycare is necessary for a child's development in the same way that some kind of formal education is necessary for a seven year old? It also plays on the insecurities of parents who don't use formal care settings – is this akin to truancy? Is it neglectful to deprive a child of institutional early-education experiences from the age of six months?

There is much evidence to suggest children would benefit from starting formal schooling at a later age. Leading Australian parenting and child development expert, Maggie Dent, has argued extensively that starting formal schooling at the age of five equates to 'stealing a year of their childhood'. It's worth noting the drawbacks of starting school before children are developmentally ready are much more freely discussed than the drawbacks of starting childcare earlier. The push to earlier schooling mirrors that of earlier daycare attendance and both are economically motivated while failing to account for the long-term costs of placing children in environments they are not developmentally equipped to be in.

Transparent discussions around childcare and the benefits of entering formal early-learning settings at later ages is considered inflammatory, where similar discussions around later school-starting ages are more palatable. Perhaps in an attempt to appeal to a broad audience, Dent does not publicly weigh in on the potential harm of early and extensive use of childcare. Because the school starting age is largely mandated and not so much a personal decision, her commentary can only be seen as an attack on the system rather than individual decisions. The use of early education is sometimes a personal decision, but so often there is very little choice due to financial stress, existing family policy frameworks, and lack of community or support. Because of the lack of choice, childcare use is effectively mandated. Any discussion about the potential negative effects of early childcare exposure must always be interpreted as an attack on the system—particularly a system in which parents aren't given transparent information—not on the parents who use that system.

So, while this might seem like merely semantics, over time the language we use informs our views and beliefs and ultimately infiltrates research agendas. The term 'educators' and 'Early Childhood Education and Care' to encompass daycare and preschool for children from birth to five years of age, are now used widely throughout research. This colours our readings of the findings, distorts actual findings, frequently leads to the measurement of academic skills only, and fails to control for age at entry. With this in mind, let's move on to other aspects of daycare research.

To properly understand the childcare environment today we need to understand how it emerged historically. Formal childcare in Australia has progressed over a century from small nurseries for disadvantaged babies to community- and publicly-run preschools for three to five year olds to a large sector made up mostly of for-profit businesses catering from babies to five year olds for extended hours. Childcare has come to be a vital part of society and it will continue to play an important role in supporting families, facilitating access to the paid workforce, choice for women and, in some instances, supporting children's development.

However, there are some important respects in which we have misunderstood and misused childcare as a tool at our disposal. Clear information about the appropriate and beneficial use of childcare has been confused by issues of facilitating gender equality, and political motivation to increase female workforce participation. We have overestimated what childcare can achieve for children in order to accommodate and justify the increasing use of it.

Childcare research as a field of study has a long and complex history. Up until the 1990s, childcare consisted mainly of model intervention daycare programs for children under three or large-scale, part-time preschool settings for children over three. Model programs were unlike the centre-based daycare settings, or 'everyday' childcare we see today. Model interventions randomly targeted disadvantaged children from infancy and resembled somewhat of a 'life transplant'. The children were provided full-time daycare with educators, doctors and nurses on site, home visits and parent education and nutritional intervention. They often included antenatal and postnatal care interventions for mothers. They were small scale, high quality, and produced significant positive effects compared to the disadvantaged children who did not undergo treatment.

Nordic countries such as Norway, Sweden, Finland, Denmark and Iceland were among the first to roll out preschool settings at scale. In the 1970s, laws were introduced in these countries that legally entitled children access to preschool. These 'universal entitlements' often didn't extend to younger than three and some involved part-time attendance, such as 20-hour entitlements in Finland for three to six year olds. These 'universal' entitlements were still subject to a work test, meaning parents in paid work were entitled to more hours. These were publicly delivered preschool settings that enjoyed sustained high levels of government investment required to expand to the general population and retain good quality care. They were accompanied by long, paid parental leave periods of around six-12 months and also often substantial home-care allowances. In Norway today, a Cash for Care allowance of around $1000 AUD per month is available for families who do not use daycare.

Daycare places were not routinely offered to all one year olds in Norway until around 2007[57]. Despite this entitlement, the proportion of one-year-old children receiving Cash-for-Care benefits has been relatively stable at around about 55%[58] as parents use it to stretch their time with their toddlers or while waiting to be offered a daycare place. This is down from 1999 when Home Care Allowances were more substantial and 73% of all parents of one to two year olds received the Cash for Care allowance. Based on the data today, around half of one year olds in Norway may not actually be entering daycare settings until they are closer to two years of age.

Due to rapid changes in the way childcare has been delivered over the decades, and the diversity of settings globally, the data for childhood outcomes following recent trends in more intensive daycare attendance patterns and at younger ages in a variety of systems is severely lacking.

Earlier data around childhood outcomes following the introduction of the Cash for Care benefits was unreliable due to immigrant families being considerably overrepresented in the sample of families that used the Home-Care Allowance. It was often criticised as slowing immigrant mothers' return to work, resulting in poorer language development for children, and reducing the overall labour-market participation of immigrant mothers. The robustness of the research in relation to childhood outcomes was inadequate because poorer outcomes found in Cash for Care cohorts were most likely a result of disadvantage arising from immigration rather than a home-care environment. Childcare could well be an effective way of addressing the disadvantage that can arise from immigrant backgrounds, alongside outreach programs and community-based playgroups.

In 2007, a law was introduced that required immigrant families to have been living in Norway for at least five years prior to having children in order to access the Cash for Care Scheme. Researchers used this as an opportunity to measure the extent to which the Cash for Care Allowance had been inhibiting labour-force participation. They found that after the law changed and immigrant uptake of HCA dropped considerably, there was no impact on labour-force participation or fertility rates. The only observable change was that these families were poorer and as a result, more disadvantaged. Mothers were choosing to continue in caregiving roles even if the state no longer supported their contribution.

In Australia, we chronically underestimate the importance of the detailed and extensive parental rights and supports as a vital part of Nordic early-childhood systems. In building high-quality early-learning settings for children before school, Norway did not abandon the importance of supporting parents to parent. The system positions parents as allies in the common goal of optimal childhood experiences. Norway effectively uses parent care to delay age at entry to daycare and thus reduce pressure on the quality systems they provide. Daycare—the care of infants and toddlers—is the most intensive form of institutional care and the most difficult to provide at scale.

Mothers are entitled to 12 months of paid parental leave at 100% of their average salary. This includes a lengthy period of shared paid leave that either parent can take – a combined parental leave of 49 weeks at 100% paid or 59 weeks at 80%[58]. Mothers in Norway who do not meet the activity test are entitled to a lump sum payment of around $12000 AUD after the birth of their child. Either parent also has a statutory right to take an additional 12 months unpaid leave.

These benefits provided by the state welfare department are in addition to private sector statutory parental-leave requirements. Mothers are entitled to nine weeks of paid maternity leave, starting three weeks before delivery and lasting until six weeks postpartum. Fathers are entitled to two weeks of unpaid paternity leave following a partner's delivery.

A surprising and rarely talked about aspect of the childcare systems in Norway, held up repeatedly as the gold standard, is that it has not closed the socioeconomic achievement gaps. Socioeconomic disparities in Norway continue to widen, although it is still possible their early-learning settings have slowed the rate at which that may otherwise have happened. Norway's approach to the early years has closed gender-equality gaps quite effectively, but a persistent pay gap exists due to stubborn patterns of highly-gendered occupations. It's also possible that a great deal of progress is attributable to parental supports other than childcare access.

A considerable degree of caution is required when considering Nordic early-childcare systems and how they have set up their 'village' due to the vastly different policy ecosystems and interactions that exist. Even the landmass size and geographic features of Australia mean childcare systems that might work well in Norway don't translate as well to our country. We are more spread out and have greater remote areas resulting in inequitable access to uniform systems like childcare.

Norway's childcare and family-policy framework has been built over many decades and informed by socialist approaches to public investment in the early years, while countries like Australia have tended towards liberal and individualistic approaches to family life. As much as we want to here in Australia, we can't just flick a switch and undo decades of private investment, commercial interests, and individualist approaches that have informed the development of our own childcare sector. Mistakes were made, people were ill-informed, and now we are dealing with the repercussions.

We must also exercise caution when examining longitudinal research that tracks children's outcomes as a result of early-learning settings they experienced decades ago in foreign countries. These early-learning experiences often do not reflect the quality of care, attendance patterns, or the age ranges we have in Australian childcare today.

Caution is also required when observing short-term outcomes. Improving reading or math scores at age five or even 10 may sound good on paper, but it is not necessarily indicative of lasting benefits. School quality and other life factors can neutralise any advances made in preschool or daycare. Cognitive benefits have a tendency to fade over time.

When we considered the research, we noted that factors such as behaviour, physical and mental health into adulthood or life satisfaction were often not measured, while also being shown to be more likely to have life-long impacts. Positive or negative behaviours and socioemotional measures were more likely to last into adulthood than academic scores. Even factors like income and finishing a college degree can only take us part way to understanding the value of a person's eventual contribution to society and their quality of life.

A key challenge in childcare research has been experimental validity and methodology. Isolating the childcare exposure as the cause of a measured benefit or negative effect is particularly difficult because children's lives are made up of so many variables that cannot be controlled or even measured. Most studies that measure behaviours like aggression are self-reported, relying on teachers and sometimes even parents to report behaviours. Parents are incredibly biased when it comes to their own kids and that makes these studies somewhat unreliable.

Studies that measure long-term behaviour outcomes in a reliable way are rare. The transition to universal childcare in Quebec in the 1980s offers some of the most clear and reliable insights into behavioural impacts of childcare that was frequently found to be low quality. In this case, characteristics such as behaviour and mental health were measured into adulthood by healthcare professionals. This is important because the subjective reporting on harder-to-measure factors could be carried out by more neutral or reliable sources.

Researchers have used all sorts of measures, controls, and analyses to glean varied and often opposing findings from the same set of numbers. They have theorised about self-selection skewing the samples and accounting for both positive and negative outcomes found in childcare studies. While better control measures have been introduced over time, many researchers continue to discount positive findings as a result of the fact that more advantaged families are more likely to use childcare and also more likely to use higher-quality care. Figures clearly back this up in Australia – the most disadvantaged families are least likely to enrol in early-learning settings while children from highly-educated, high-income families are more likely to have higher attendance at better-quality centres.

The skewed sample theory is more often used to explain away the childcare studies that show exposure has resulted in negative developmental outcomes. Zachrissen and Dearing[59] theorise that families of children with behavioural problems are simply more likely to use more childcare because they need more of a break from the behaviour. It has been argued that, aside from balloted selection into model intervention programs, randomised control trials that could overcome self-selection problems are almost impossible to carry out in relation to childcare.

Childcare literature as a body of research is ripe for manipulation to suit the policy aim or ideology of your choosing. The evidence is so mixed that you can find a particular study to 'prove' myriad points on any given day. You can even pluck only the positive findings from within a study, and omit the negative findings and study limitations, as we saw in the Productivity Commission's recent review of the literature[60].

The review referenced a study of children aged between one and two attending a French creche, which found that creche two year olds could say 80 words, which was 12 more on average than two year olds cared for at home. This reference was made as evidence that 'attending daycare between the ages of 1 and 2 was found to significantly improve language development'. What the literature review failed to mention was that the study also found increased behavioural problems at age two.

At first glance, these findings might seem meaningful for Australian parents with children in daycare under the age of three but if we dig a little deeper, the situation is a lot more complex. Daycares in France are state run and funded, and report homogenous high-quality care standards. This is in contrast to Australian daycares that are 80% run for-profit with more variable quality of care. The second issue is that behaviour and vocabulary measures were self-reported by parents regardless of the care arrangement. Parents aren't always totally reliable narrators when it comes to their own children.

Finally, what does having 12 more words at two years of age mean in the big picture? Can this really be considered a 'significant improvement'? The measurements stop at two, and without multiple continued measurements we are unable to determine the rate of word acquisition – a more accurate indication of future cognitive ability. It's also important to note that the standard range for a two-year-olds' vocabulary is between 50 and 200 words, so while children in parental care had fewer words, they were still well within the standard range.

In a similar sense, it's impossible to know if a toddler exhibiting slightly poorer behaviour than their peers is going to experience life-long disadvantage as a result. Although behavioural impacts at an early age have been shown in other research to have more lasting effects than academic impacts, these findings don't necessarily translate to this particular study.

The self-selection of samples was a problem in this study, with higher-income families more likely to enrol in creche, while lower-income families were overrepresented in the home-care group and most likely to have children with a low birth weight.

Another general concern we have with the validity of childcare literature is that most people who work in childcare research may overestimate the role of formal education settings due to confirmation bias – they already believe childcare is beneficial and are simply aiming to prove that. They might also have a pre-existing affiliation with school and education settings that eventually lead them to research in this area. In the same way doctors have a tendency to medicalise any issue, people with education backgrounds tend to 'educationalise' issues and examine the literature with this in mind. From the data, we can infer that academia is overrepresented by highly-educated people who are also most likely to use childcare for their children and may develop a confirmation bias over time.

For all of these reasons, we must interpret complex data sets with care. We must understand that many of our policy decisions over the years have been based on flawed data or research not relevant to our situation. To be frank, we simply don't have solid data on the effects of current Australian childcare systems. We are experimenting and this is unacceptable. We must urgently set about implementing and properly funding new research and monitoring programs that will be critical to informing policies relating to early childhood in the future.

CHAPTER TEN

What Can Daycare Research Tell Us?

Considering the many limitations of daycare research discussed in the previous chapter, I find it most helpful to examine the literature broadly, identifying patterns that have reliably emerged over half a century of childcare research in a variety of contexts, including those which can be more safely applied to an Australian sociopolitical context. The body of research on the whole does tell an important story and follows certain patterns that appear to be quite universal. Effect sizes of attending childcare from birth to five are almost always larger for disadvantaged children, whether they are positive or negative. Disadvantaged children have the most to gain from the compensatory effect of childcare but only if it is higher quality relative to home-care quality. Disadvantaged children also appear to be more sensitive to poor-quality care in many cases.

There is a serious dearth of evidence that shows children who are not disadvantaged can benefit from exposure to daycare settings, that is childcare delivered under the age of three. The extremely limited number of studies that have found benefits for under-threes are concentrated in Europe, particularly Nordic regions. There are also studies that show negative impacts. We feel the inability to reliably establish benefits for children under three who are not disadvantaged—without coexisting negative outcomes, which may offset the gains and in sociopolitical contexts that more closely reflect Australia—means we are required to exercise serious caution when considering the scale and intensity of exposure to daycare for children under three.

The other pattern that has emerged most clearly since we began measuring the impacts of early-learning settings is that older children seem to benefit more reliably than younger children. In preschool settings it's still disadvantaged children that have the most to gain. There are Australian studies that have found no improvement in NAPLAN scores after preschool attendance[61], and other studies that have found small, cognitive improvements related to preschool which extend broadly.

Longitudinal studies measuring the impacts of childcare are relatively scarce and in their infancy in Australia. They are struggling to establish evidence that everyday childcare is improving outcomes in a meaningful way. The E4Kids study began tracking 2500 children aged three in 2008. It is 'the most extensive longitudinal study ever conducted into the impact and effectiveness of early childhood education and care in Australia, as well as outcomes for children who do not attend programs.'[62] It's the most important data we have for an Australian context, yet the least publicised – why? Because the research was unable to establish the benefits of childcare.

The E4Kids 2016 report found strong correlations between family socioeconomic status and Grade 3 NAPLAN scores. It found similar correlations between home-learning environment and NAPLAN scores. The study found no relationship between children's verbal ability and the type of ECEC program attended; the mathematical ability of children cared for at home exceeded that of children who attended formal childcare. There was also no evidence that exposure to everyday ECEC acted to narrow achievement gaps related to socioeconomic status and instead found developmental gaps widened due to more advantaged families accessing higher-quality care. The study did control for family characteristics and baseline abilities of children at the beginning of monitoring. It did not control for quality of the centre or actual dosage, though it did measure how many years before starting school a child entered childcare.

On the other hand, small and non-intensive interventions in home-learning environments, which included educating parents on how best to support their child's development, was shown to have positive effects. The study also found bilingual children benefited from kindergarten programs in terms of language development but the same effect was not found in other formal childcare settings. 'There are two main findings which emerge if ECEC programs are to make an independent contribution to improving children's learning and development outcomes. The first is how to improve the quality of the programs ... the second is how to ensure that children from disadvantaged backgrounds enter programs that demonstrate high quality teacher-child interactions...'

The report found the reason for the lack of impact was due to low levels of instructional support found in 99% of centres. Instructional support is talking to children while they play, and rich verbal back-and-forth interactions are key mechanisms for improving cognitive development. The paper recommended 'comprehensive targeted services in the least advantaged areas, with a particular focus on access to quality programs for the youngest children from disadvantaged backgrounds'.

In 2024, the Productivity Commission, as part of an Inquiry into rolling out universal childcare in Australia, put together an extensive literature review that examined the evidence base around the potential positive or negative impacts of childcare. The literature review supported the two main patterns in childcare outcomes: high-quality care can have positive outcomes but overwhelmingly these positive outcomes occur only for preschool-aged children and/or children from abusive, neglectful, or impoverished homes.

Of around 49 research papers referenced, just a handful featured findings pertaining to children under the age of two or three. Many papers looked at the evidence of part-time preschool over shorter days – around six-hours long[63]. Papers found both positive and negative impacts, though the negative impacts were often omitted. This occurred when referencing Havnes and Mogstad's work[64] in studying the effects of Norwegian expansion of universal childcare. 'We find that most of the gains in earnings associated with the universal childcare program relate to children of low-income parents, whereas upper-class children actually experience a loss in earnings', the researchers clearly stated. 'Our context is a reform from late-1975 in Norway, which led to a large-scale expansion of subsidized childcare. All children 3–6 years old were eligible regardless of their parents' employment and marital status, and available childcare slots were in general allocated according to length of time on the waiting list. The reform we study led to a staged expansion of subsidized childcare, across Norway's more than 400 municipalities.'

In this instance, a study examining the rollout of subsidised preschool, which actually found a loss in earnings for children from wealthy families, is repeatedly referenced to support the rollout of universal childcare from birth in Australia.

Chetty's[65] work from 2011 is used as evidence that not all 'childcare effects' fade when the actual study appears to be measuring the effects of a primary school intervention. 'Students who were randomly assigned to higher-quality classrooms in grades K–3— as measured by classmates' end-of-class test scores—have higher earnings, college attendance rates, and other outcomes.'

Research looking at the Headstart program in Tennessee, US[66], was a preschool program aimed at disadvantaged children. To this day, eligibility for this program is largely income-based and the program is mostly only open to children from families living below the poverty line. The study found 'The long-term impact for disadvantaged children is large despite "fadeout" of test score gains.'

The PC review also referenced the Perry Preschool – a preschool program (3-4 year olds) targeted at disadvantaged families in the 1960s in the US[67]. One of Heckman and Kautz's 2012 studies[68] is not peer reviewed, but all references relate to preschool programs for disadvantaged children and early primary programs.

Silliman and Mäkinen's 2022[69] study is repeatedly referenced despite measuring the effects of changes to the Finland daycare law in 1973, which granted three to seven year olds universal access to 20 hours per week. Children could get full-time preschool access if parents met the activity test and, once again, it finds the most significant gains for low-income families.

Again and again we see this all the way through the Productivity Commission's literature review, which is concurrently making claims such as 'ECEC programs have produced benefits across a wide range of outcomes', and 'ECEC programs have produced a persistent increase in employment and earnings, improvement over various developmental and cognitive domains...' Based on the reference sources, these claims are a complete overestimate at best, untrue at worst.

In the end, I could only find two studies in the entire review that related to babies and toddlers in childcare, who were not necessarily disadvantaged. One study by Gruber et al 2023[70], which wasn't peer reviewed, related specifically to children under three. This study found that children whose mothers accessed Finland's Home Care Allowance rather than going to childcare were more likely to have a conviction and less likely to attend college. The findings cannot be applied to an Australian context and used to justify major childcare policy changes as long as it remained unreviewed and unpublished.

A study by Barschkett in 2022[71] is also referenced as evidence that an expansion of CBDC for children under the age of three in Germany 'reduced doctor visits, healthcare costs and diagnoses of behavioural and emotional disorders, as well as, for children experiencing disadvantage, obesity.'

The study did not find this at all. Barschkett writes in his conclusion:

'Specifically, I find that early daycare attendance increases the prevalence of respiratory and infectious diseases and healthcare consumption when entering daycare (1-2 years) by 5-6%. At elementary school age (6-10 years), the prevalence decreases by similar magnitudes. I do not find evidence for an effect of daycare attendance on mental disorders, obesity, injuries, vision problems, or healthcare costs. Heterogeneity analysis indicates more pronounced effects for children from disadvantaged areas, earlier detection of vision problems, and a reduction in obesity in these children.'

It's shocking that such a serious misreading of the evidence could fly under the radar, go undetected, in a government inquiry.

Another used to support claims that childcare could benefit one year olds was the 2021 Cattan et al., study[72] of the Sure Start program in the UK. The study found an increase of hospitalisation by 10% when entering daycare at the age of one, but then later reduced hospitalisations for those children between 11 and 15. Benefits were once again concentrated in disadvantaged cohorts with effects entirely null for 30% of the most advantaged children. The benefits that were detected cannot be linked to daycare attendance alone as this program also included ante and postnatal care. This is also a longitudinal study dating back to 1990 where researchers concluded that 'Findings speak to importance of integrating health services, early education and care, and parenting services to promote child development in a holistic way.'

Sure Start was in almost no ways comparable to the for-profit daycare centres run in Australia today, yet it was deemed relevant for the Productivity Commission's purposes. It's also unclear from the study at what age this cohort entered daycare, because there is information to suggest that Sure Start early-learning programs were only offered for children two to three years and older. The rest of the services were parent/child development and support services. It's well documented that the program's effectiveness declined as it was expanded beyond the most disadvantaged children.

The review repeatedly referenced several studies with positive findings from expanding access to preschool-aged children[73].

The Productivity Commission claimed to find evidence that proved age at enrolment and intensity of childcare attendance did not matter to childhood outcomes. When you actually read the studies they reference in relation to this, the liberties that have been taken are clear. For example, van Huizen and Plantenga, 2018[74], used to support the conclusion that age of enrolment in daycare doesn't matter, actually wrote: 'Although it is frequently claimed that participation in child care and preschool improves child development and leads to positive outcomes in the long run, the overall evidence on universal ECEC is somewhat mixed: About a third of the estimates indicates positive impacts on children's outcomes, half of the estimates are insignificant and the rest are negative.

'Age of enrolment into universal ECEC is not a major factor in explaining the impact – that is mostly explained by quality and because benefits are concentrated in low socioeconomic children. Public programs provide more favourable evidence than private.'

What they failed to point out is age at enrolment has not been found to be a major factor because there is a complete dearth of studies that control for age of enrolment. Also, babies attending daycare at large scale is a relatively new phenomenon where the effects are yet unable to be captured in longitudinal research.

Evans et al., 2024[75] do make a finding that CBDC is almost equally likely to produce benefits for enrolment under or over three in middle- to low-income countries, which Australia is not.

A study from Japan[76] found that childcare enrolment at two and half years—hardly applicable to a nine month old—improved language development and reduced the symptoms of inattention, hyperactivity, and aggression among the children of low-education mothers.

Another study from Norway (Zachrisson et al. 2023[77]), concluded, 'We find the scale-up of ECEC starting in the second year of life improved test scores, especially for children from families with low levels of parental education.' Researchers also tempered this finding, stating, 'large and persistent (even increasing) achievement gaps in Norway suggests that there are substantial limitations to what an educational system can achieve in equalizing opportunity.'

In order to discount a large body of research finding negative behavioural impacts of childcare, such as the US NICHD meta-analysis, various cortisol studies and the series of studies conducted on the Quebec childcare program (discussed in more detail below), the Productivity Commission introduced the study by Dearing and Zachrisson 2017 (referenced in the previous chapter) that claims children with behavioural problems are overrepresented in childcare settings.

Often, studies referenced in support of universal childcare actually conclude the opposite of universality, clearly stating disadvantaged children must be prioritised. For example, Yazejian et al., 2015[78], found, 'Results suggest that renewed focus is needed on ensuring that children at risk for poor school outcomes have access to high-quality EEC early in life and for sustained periods of time to reduce later achievement gaps.'

Finally, the Productivity Commission scratch-around for evidence to prove there is no such thing as 'too much childcare'. This was a negligent point for the PC to make based on conflicting, scarce evidence that fails to control for age at enrolment. To suggest that evidence supports the idea that a one year old can attend daycare seven days a week without negative impacts is a complete stretch of the imagination. Most of the studies referenced focused on low-income families and whether there was any harm in increased attendance for low-income families. There is little or no consideration of age at enrolment. Several studies referenced in support of the claim that higher attendance isn't harmful were looking at preschool-aged children[79].

One meta-analysis in 2023[80] found no association between hours in centre-based care and externalising problems. On the surface, this supports an argument for universal childcare but on a complete reading, the strength of this meta-analysis quickly fades. This meta-analysis failed to control for age at entry to care, with studies examined looking at a range of enrolment ages from five months old to three years. It didn't control for the kind of care delivered – the childcare settings included a range of models from for-profit to state-funded or state-regulated. The analysis also included studies that looked exclusively at disadvantaged cohorts.

Limitations noted by the authors themselves include the short-term nature of the findings. Researchers were clear they had no findings relating to possible long-term harm. They were also clear that the null association was found for this particular set of studies, but associations may have emerged in different study sets.

One study referenced by the PC actually contradicts the claim for which it is referenced, that higher attendance is more beneficial[81]. Authors wrote, 'we find that there are initial benefits for students and the mothers of students who attend full-day kindergarten, but that these differences largely evaporate by third grade. Contrary to claims by some advocates, attending full-day kindergarten is found to have no additional benefit for students in families with income below the poverty threshold.'

A German study[82] of three to six year olds found negative effects of more preschool attendance for most children, with positive academic impacts only for migrant children. The authors wrote, 'we find that more hours have a negative effect on children's socio-emotional well-being. Subgroup analysis suggests that this result is driven by children from disadvantaged family backgrounds, especially those from low-education backgrounds, single-parent households and migrant families. On a brighter note, we find that full-day care has a positive effect on the school readiness of immigrant children.'

In a full-day universal kindergarten study[82], the authors are clear about the marginal size of positive effects found, 'Our point estimates for the average effect of FDK on achievement are mostly positive, occasionally statistically significant, and always small. The effect is substantially larger among students who speak English as a second language, a result that is consistent with prior findings.'

I've examined the Productivity Commission's literature review at length because this is emblematic of how childcare research is often presented – it is cherry picked, negative findings are explained away, positive findings are blown out of proportion. Findings are often blatantly misrepresented. People want so badly for childcare to be the solution that a strong confirmation bias often characterises the representation of the research or the research itself.

The vast majority of people who read this literature review would be undoubtedly left with the impression that childcare is beneficial for all children in an Australian context; however, a closer reading of the actual papers referenced tells a very different story. The findings for positive and negative impacts are tenuous, fraught with design and robustness issues, often unable to be translated to lifelong benefits, politicised and contaminated by confirmation bias. Absolute caution must be exercised in the reading of research and the representation of research, especially where it is being used to inform policy that will dictate children's exposure to these settings.

Because of the ambiguity of the findings and the difficulty in drawing clear conclusions, we cannot continue to give childcare policy the 'benefit of the doubt'. When it comes to the wellbeing of children and families, this is now an ethical issue. We cannot continue to knowingly increase exposure to settings without absolute confirmation that it will be beneficial, or at least not harmful.

Curiously, the Productivity Commission failed to mention childcare cortisol studies or the childcare meta-analysis from the United States' National Institute of Child Health and Human Development. It also did not include a rigorous analysis of research exploring child outcomes after the implementation of universal childcare in the Quebec province of Canada. These longitudinal datasets are some of the most comprehensive and revealing data we have on the impacts of childcare, particularly in the long run. American and Canadian childcare systems closely reflect our own and any data coming from these countries should be closely analysed by our policy makers.

The Quebec childcare program was introduced in 1997 to provide universal, affordable daycare for children in the province. The program provided daycare positions at a flat rate of $5 per day regardless of parental income. Because the program was rolled out in Quebec and not in other provinces in Canada, it provides an incredibly large-scale natural experiment. The program quite clearly increased maternal labour force participation; however, a series of subsequent studies found negative impacts on children's outcomes. In particular, the studies revealed that children who participated in the program experienced worse health, lower life satisfaction, and higher crime rates later in life compared to other children in Canada where the program was not introduced. The children in the program also showed lower non-cognitive skills such as emotional regulation and social behaviour, relative to other children in other provinces. There was also evidence that the program led to more hostile, less consistent parenting, worse parental health, and lower-quality parental relationships[83].

The same criticisms of the pro-childcare studies apply to studies that uncover negative findings. Are there confounding factors related to early childhood development that the Quebec studies do not control for? Yes. For example, quality of parent care, quality of childcare, type of childcare. The studies also compare children from different localities, which could bring a whole host of other variables other than a difference in childcare policy. Many of the findings are based on self-reported characteries; for example, a parent or a caregiver rating a behavioural issue. Is it still cause for concern that a whole generation of children from a particular Canadian province appear to have experienced a decline in a range of outcomes after universal childcare was implemented? Absolutely.

The PC report addressed the Quebec studies and essentially explained away the negative findings on the basis that it is likely that the quality of the care experienced by children was poor (for example, all the educators did not have the specified qualifications), because of the rapid roll-out of the program, and because the expansion was driven by for-profit providers rather than not-for-profit providers. These are arguably not dissimilar conditions to those in which Australia is now operating, noting the rapid expansion of for-profit operators in recent years (of the 300 to 400 new childcare centres opening each year, 95% are for-profit) and the significant number of childcare centres failing to meet regulatory standards[84].

The National Institute of Child Health and Development (NICHD) study, which the PC report did not address, commenced in 1990 and is one of the most comprehensive longitudinal studies ever undertaken. It looked at more than 1,100 children from across ten US cities and compared factors such as care quality and care quantity (including number of hours spent in childcare and age of entry) between maternal care and non-maternal care (including, variously, care by fathers, grandparents, nannies, and commercial childcare centres).

The study found a variety of results. One finding was that longer hours in non-maternal care impacted on mother-infant attunement and sensitivity, including that more time in care predicted less harmonious mother-infant interaction and less sensitive mothering, regardless of the quality of the care. The study also found that by age four-and-a-half, three times as many children (17%) in over thirty hours of care showed more aggressive behavioural problems than children in care for fewer than ten hours. This was regardless of the quality of care, and variables such as parent attributes were taken into account. This study, too, is complex and nuanced. It also found high-quality childcare was associated with better pre-academic skills and language performance. Nonetheless, the study concludes that family characteristics were essentially the most important influence and played a more significant role than the childcare option used[85].

More recently, a cortisol study that sampled 320 toddlers in Norway, published in 2024, made several key findings, including that "[t]here were no differences between morning cortisol levels in childcare and morning cortisol levels at home. In childcare, children showed a significant rise in cortisol levels between morning and afternoon. At home, children showed a significant decline in cortisol levels between morning and afternoon. Afternoon cortisol levels were significantly lower at home than in childcare." The study also found that "[y]ounger children (up to 26 months, below the median) had overall higher cortisol levels than older children (27 months and older, at or above the median). In addition, older children showed a steeper decline of cortisol levels at home. Children in groups with more than three children per caregiver had slightly, yet significantly, higher cortisol levels in childcare and slightly lower cortisol levels at home. Children in classrooms with a higher classroom disorganization score had distinctly higher cortisol levels in childcare and slightly higher cortisol levels in the afternoon at home."

Overall, the researchers suggested the results indicated that toddlers probably are somewhat stressed in childcare and that the childcare context may be more difficult to navigate for younger toddlers than older toddlers, in particular because toddlers probably find the prolonged absence of parents challenging[86].

A meta-analysis (Vermeer) in 2006 made similar findings, but to see these findings repeated as recently as 2024 is cause for concern. A finder of higher cortisol levels in daycare compared to at home has been reliably reproduced since 1982, yet policy has not responded to this at all. These studies lack a longitudinal follow-up to establish the long-term impacts of these elevated cortisol levels associated with daycare attendance. We don't know that these elevated levels of cortisol are 'too much' per se.

This book is not meant to be an exhaustive list of research papers. There are thousands on either side of the debate and it is very difficult to find a consensus position. The point of this part of the book is to show that a conservative approach is necessary when childcare continues to be an experimental approach. This chapter is intended to challenge the current discourse and show how easily an unfounded narrative can be built up and accepted as fact by many people who do not have the time, resources, or the inclination to challenge it. I encourage you to do your own reading.

It's not just childcare research specifically that must be considered when tackling this issue, particularly given the inherent complexity of seeking to measure the impacts of childcare attendance on outcomes across a person's life. Perhaps the strongest evidence emerges when we consider child developmental research more broadly as we have done throughout this book. What do we know about how mental health issues or developmental delays arise in young children, what do we know causes distress or toxic stress in young children, and do known features of childcare serve to alleviate or exacerbate this? We can apply our knowledge from neuroscience, biological, and even anthropological fields to better understand whether group care settings, high caregiver turnover and absence of parents, is developmentally appropriate for babies and toddlers.

For example, look at what the evidence base tells us about how emotional regulation develops in young children[87]. The part of the brain that enables us to regulate our own emotions is not fully developed in babies and young children. Infants and young children rely on a caregiver who is attuned to them to consistently and effectively help them regulate their emotions. In plain terms, when young children get upset they need help to calm down. If that help is not available, if there is not someone in close proximity who can reliably regulate them, they risk remaining in a heightened state of anxiety for extended periods.

For most children, the person who knows them, who they have a positive relationship with, and who can reliably and effectively calm them when they are upset, is a parent. A formative sense of security is attached to a parent. This is not to say parents are the only people who can do this for a child, but they are usually the most effective emotional regulators of their children. Over months and years of being the person helping the child, the child develops an association with that figure. It can be the presence of the caregiver alone that enables a child to stay emotionally regulated.

The caregiver must routinely and consistently meet the needs of the child so that an association can develop that the caregiver is a source of comfort and security. If this relationship is interrupted or the caregiver, for whatever reason, is unreliable in their ability to help a baby or child emotionally regulate, the attachment may be insufficient to promote healthy psychological development.

In this sense, research uncovering the biological basis of attachment theory and emotional regulation[88], gives us a good idea of when childcare is and is not developmentally optimal. Care settings that involve stressed and overworked caregivers or a high turnover of caregivers or an absence of key emotional regulators such as parents, would likely result in conditions that are harmful for child development.

Another example would be applying evidence that demonstrates emotional and intellectual learning occurs optimally in a calm and relaxed state when the parasympathetic nervous system dominates. If time in childcare has been associated with an activated sympathetic nervous system, for instance in the cortisol studies, this will likely not provide an optimal developmental environment.

Similarly, it is relevant to consider studies that examine childcare practices from an evolutionary perspective. We lived as hunter-gatherers for the vast majority of our evolutionary history. Looking at the practices of contemporary hunter-gatherers can give some hints as to the whether current daycare conditions are aligned with the conditions to which human children are psychologically adapted. In other words, are there particular forms of childcare that are aligned with our evolved psychology and therefore optimal for development?

One example of such a study was published in 2024 by Dr Nikhil Chaudry and two co-authors. They examined the caregiving practices of infants and toddlers (0–4 years old) among Mbendjele hunter-gatherers in the Northern Republic of Congo, and the level of sensitive responsiveness by carers towards those infants and toddlers[89]. Based on their observations, the researchers suggested that young children may be evolutionarily primed to expect 'exceptionally high levels of physical contact and care, swift soothing responses to their crying, and personal attention from several caregivers beyond their biological parents' and further suggested that this did not align with the experience of children in modern daycare settings, in which children are cared for by a low ratio of adults to children. To minimise risks to wellbeing, the authors recommend that higher caregiver-to-child ratios should be implemented in daycare settings together with greater stability of key caregivers.

In an earlier study, Dr Chaudry and Dr Swanepoel identify that 'The communal living [of hunter gatherers] results in a high ratio of available caregivers to infants/toddlers, often exceeding 10:1. This contrasts starkly with the nuclear family unit, and even more so with nursery settings, which according to Department of Education regulations require ratios of 1:3 or 1:4.'[90]

Again, interpreting the results of research of this kind is not without complexity. In particular, it cannot be assumed that mismatches between our evolved psychological adaptations and our modern-day experiences of daycare necessarily lead to poorer outcomes; it may be the case that the relevant child-development aspects are phenotypically plastic (flexible).

It is childcare research combined with evidence from other fields that has led credible experts[91] to argue that long periods of time in institutional childcare is not in the best interests of small children, including Dr Allan Schore[92], psychologist, neuropsychology researcher and author; Penelope Leach[92], child psychologist and author of *Your Baby and Child* and *Child Care Today*; Erica Komisar[92], psychoanalyst and author of *Being There;* Dr Peter Cook[92], child and adult psychiatrist, and author of *Mothering Matters*; and Steve Biddulph AM[93], psychologist and internationally-renowned parent educator, and author of *Raising Boys, The Secret of Happy Children*, and *Raising Girls*.

Experts in attachment theory such as Gordon Neufeld PhD[94], clinical psychologist and author of *Hold Onto Your Kids*, discuss the benefits of close physical and emotional attachment with parental figures, particularly in the early years of children's lives.

The extent to which the government has manipulated and ignored the evidence in pursuit of its own economic agendas, is disturbing. A stark example of the position the government has taken on childcare played out on our television screens in 2023.

Childcare is 'Good for Children, Good for Australia' claimed the ad, funded and authorised by the Australian Government, Canberra. This campaign crossed a line. It told us that government has accepted an absolute affirmative position in respect to childcare and is no longer receptive to evidence. But perhaps more concerning is the extent to which this ad misled families who are trying to make the best decision for their kids. It was a carefully controlled message using obvious marketing tactics to convey a particular rosy image of childcare.

The ad shows Mia, a child of about four, giddy with joy and running to the car to get on her way to daycare. The sun is shining, her eyes are bright, and the snotty tissues are nowhere to be seen. It's quite a departure from the reality families face each day as they take much younger children or babies—who can be tearful, tired or sick—to daycare. The sleek and soothing female voice-over matter-of-factly explains that childcare "helps more children like Mia develop their learning and social skills". Mia is also conveniently of an age group we feel far more comfortable with out-of-home-care settings.

No prizes for guessing why the visuals of this campaign don't show newborn babies heading off to spend the day in a for-profit childcare centre. Or a mother trying to extricate herself from a screaming toddler at the entrance. At drop off, Mia trots off into the morning light, Astro turf under foot, with not a care in the world.

This ad encourages us to put on rose-coloured glasses when uncomfortable feelings start to rise about the suitability of childcare for babies and very young children. The ad took advantage of that vulnerability – how badly we want to believe childcare is the answer.

In a context where ads like this are playing on the TV, it's no wonder parents find themselves somewhat misinformed about the needs of babies and toddlers. This ad betrays a true willingness on the part of our leaders to grossly mislead families who are trying to make the best decision for their kids. They are purposefully feeding us a convenient delusion.

A 2015 literature review by the Australian Institute of Health and Welfare failed to draw a clear conclusion on the impacts of childcare. It found that most of the research to date is inconclusive, reporting 'attendance at childcare in the first 3 years of life has no strong effects on cognitive and language development for children who are not disadvantaged at home, provided childcare is of a high quality (CCCH 2007[95]).' The report did acknowledge that the quality of childcare is crucial in determining the impacts. 'Poor quality childcare was found to produce deficits in language and cognitive function for young children (Productivity Commission 2014[96]).'

In relation to preschool specifically, the literature review found that 'Full-time attendance at preschool led to no more significant gains than part-time attendance.' This tells us that five-day weeks for four-year-old children, proposed in the 2022 announcement of an earlier year of school in Victoria and NSW, may not actually benefit the kids developmentally or improve academic outcomes. Yet, the announcement of an extra year of school was littered with phrases like 'ensuring our children have the best start in life'. The only certainty is that a policy like this has short-term benefits for the economy.

The government seems unwilling to address a strong evidence base which demonstrates childcare in institutional settings where an unrelated caregiver is assigned to multiple babies or children is often a chronically stressful environment for children under three and does not reliably meet their development needs[97]. The consistency with which saliva cortisol tests have demonstrated stress responses in children under three in care has huge implications for public health, and demands the inclusion of this evidence base in policy development.

Chronic stress in babies and young children should be of keen interest as it occurs at a time when the brain is laying down foundational neural pathways with a large degree of permanence. The presence of chronic stress at this time can have lifelong mental health implications including an overactive stress response and difficulties regulating emotions[98]. Research has shown that 'children who experience disruptions in caretaking and attachment or who experience unresponsive or harsh parenting may be even more susceptible to the effects of cumulative risk exposure and allostatic load.[99]'

Allostatic load refers to the cumulative burden of chronic stress and life events. The stress children experience may not be immediately obvious, as Dr Andrew Garner from the American Association of Paediatrics describes "this kind of stress response in young children can lead to less visible yet permanent changes in the brain structure and function" (as paraphrased by Erica Komisar in her book *Being There*).

We are in a situation where policies encourage earlier and more intensive childcare without yet having a complete understanding of the impacts. Parents making decisions about the care of their babies and young children deserve better than this. Parents should have complete freedom to access childcare, they should also have access to transparent information that reflects the evidence base.

As a starting point, policy should be governed by the patterns outlined in the broad research. For families where abuse and neglect is an issue, access to parental education and support should be prioritised along with income support and free access to high-quality childcare and preschool. These children should be referred to childcare or the out-of-home care system at the discretion of trained social workers and family support professionals. In these situations, concurrent parental rehabilitation programs should be an ongoing priority for governments.

For families with complex needs such as disability, mental illness, behavioural and learning issues, or even multiple births, parental support should be a priority. Parents should have the freedom to decide whether that support is best delivered in the form of childcare or in-home support measures. It is unacceptable that parents who wish to provide quality care for a high-needs child, who want to better equip themselves with the skills to care for their own child, would be forced to outsource this care for financial reasons or due to lack of support from relevant services.

For low-income families, financial support must be a priority so that any choice to access free childcare is not made under duress. While circumstances of disadvantage are often found to be closely linked to income, many of these studies fail to control for other parental background characteristics such as education. As such, income alone has not always been found to be a reliable predictor of parenting quality and home environment[100].

Parental education levels are a much more reliable indicator of parenting quality, but still not a certainty as care intelligence can be much harder to measure than academic intelligence. It is essential that parents who can provide quality care are given the opportunity to do so, regardless of their income or education level. Wrap-around services can assist parents in identifying where developmental needs are not being met and how best to address this.

For middle-income families, a means-tested subsidy is sufficient to deliver any marginal developmental benefit of childcare while still enabling families to supplement their income. Beyond that, it is no longer a measure that has the child's best interests at heart or facilitates genuine choice, but simply a measure that results in short term economic benefits for families and government.

If government intends to use childcare subsidies as a proxy for financial aid, beyond what is necessary for child development, they must be clear that the policy is purely a financial aid measure. They cannot continue to claim that developmental benefits of childcare extend to an 18-month-old in full time care.

Many middle-income families are upset that I argue in favour of means-tested childcare subsidies because they are financially hurting, can't afford the things they want or need, and can think of a thousand better ways to spend the money they use on childcare. This speaks partly to our unwillingness to pay for care services, even though many of us are aware of the tireless work that goes with looking after small children. It also shows our inability to see that we deserve better than childcare subsidies and we are selling ourselves short.

If government really cared about supporting middle income parents in a cost-of-living crisis and giving kids 'best starts' they would be offering means-tested carer payments for families with children under five. Parents can use that money to access childcare if that is their preference. Instead, the support for these middle-income families is provided only on the condition that they give up precious time with their young children – for those "trading away our lives for the shallow rewards of capitalism", in Steve Biddulph's words. It's so obviously transactional, yet many of us have fallen for it hook, line and sinker. Governments can put on their superhero capes like they're saving us, but really it's just a short-term economic boost with fairly dubious child development outcomes and arguably costing governments more in the long run due to declining health outcomes.

Ideally, high-income families should be able to access centre-based childcare if that is their preference, but only once the needs of low income or otherwise disadvantaged children are being adequately met.

Universal, part-time access to high-quality preschool programs is essential regardless of socioeconomic status. Access to health services that can identify delays or behavioural issues should be universally available to families. Access to transparent information and parent education that can help families make informed decisions about care models should be universal.

CHAPTER ELEVEN

The Business of Raising Kids

If daycare is going to be part of the village going forward, it's vital we understand the business model that is currently behind this part of our village. The Australian childcare system, with for-profit operators making up 70% of centre-based daycare centres[101], has sadly become an international cautionary tale. Research shows that for-profit childcare centres consistently deliver poorer quality care than public and not-for-profit centres[102]. The number one priority for anyone who wishes to expand childcare use in Australia is to first improve the quality of childcare. If it is to become an effective substitute for parts of the social fabric that are irretrievable, the dominance of the for-profit sector simply must be addressed.

Weaning off the private equity that has built Australia's childcare system as we know it today is a complex and long-term operation. Canada is one of the only other nations setting down this path and attempting to implement universal childcare in a sector where for-profit operators hold a significant share of the market. And with for-profit operators taking up between 30-50% of said market, Canada is still only dealing with roughly half the representation we have here in Australia. Nonetheless, it might help us to examine their plans to rein in their for-profit sector and consider how this might work in Australia, where we have barely scratched the surface on this obvious starting point for improving early-childhood outcomes.

The Canadian government has identified that it is a poor and inefficient use of taxpayer funds to continue heavily subsidising a sector to the point of universal access when it is largely owned by private entities that keep raising their fees in line with subsidy increases. So, their plan is simply to constrain the growth of for-profit centres by legislating caps on their profits, auditing spending, and restricting public funds that are funnelled into them. The market restructure underway is of a smaller magnitude than we require and Canada has already been hammering away at it for years. It will take decades to rebuild the foundations of their childcare sector so that it relies mostly on public and not-for-profit funds.

Privatising childcare is notoriously difficult to undo. The Canadian government and individual provinces now find themselves in a quagmire of multilateral agreements meaning different rules for for-profits and not-for-profits in different regions. The nation, at times, becomes paralysed in a state of wanting to reduce for-profit representation but also relying on them to meet demand for new spots. Not-for-profits and state-run centres often lack the financial backing and know-how that enables aggressive expansion required to meet demand.

The world-leading, universal childcare systems that emerged in Nordic regions were built on a predominantly non-profit and state-run childcare sector from the beginning. The public sectors have enjoyed sustained high government investment and have been able to grow with the population gradually as demand built over time. These systems operate almost exclusively in childcare markets made up of less than 10% for-profit providers. The number of for-profit centres allowed to operate in these systems is planned and capped to ensure they only account for a small portion of providers. This controls the overall quality of childcare delivery.

These systems also don't provide daycare from birth, it's usually not entirely free, and most centres have shorter operating hours. These are some of the conditions that make free, high-quality and heavily-subsidised childcare a realistic, beneficial, and affordable public policy measure.

In Australia, we currently offer subsidised childcare from birth, and on this we are almost a complete international loner. In Sweden, Iceland, Norway, and Denmark it is uncommon to find a baby in a daycare centre. In Norway in 2022 just 0.9% of children in daycare were under one year old. In Australia in 2017, that figure was 30%[103], though it is likely higher now.

Preschool is more commonly free in countries with universal childcare, but most systems still require a gap payment. The subsidy rates are generally similar to our own but the difference is our fees are much higher in comparison. The problem is not our subsidy level, it's our highly-privatised and highly-profitable childcare sector. It's our decades-long legacy of actively facilitating for-profits to take over the delivery of childcare. 'Best starts for kids' and 'gender equality' has never been so lucrative. Paying subsidies to parents in a for-profit system is like endlessly patching an old, leaky water tank. You might slow the leak, but ultimately you need to replace the whole tank.

The obvious first step to universal, better-quality childcare would be to do what Canada is doing – mounting a complex market restructure, reining in the expansion of for-profits and ultimately phasing some of them out. It won't be easy, but if the government is serious about universality and quality of childcare, it's the only way. For-profits would need to be steadily replaced with public or not-for-profit centres that are given the financial backing and advisory necessary to expand in line with demand.

The next step would be implementing a proper paid parental leave system and reducing the need to use childcare under one year old. Only at the end of paid parental leave, when the child is between one and two years of age, should families become eligible for a subsidised or free position in a daycare facility. This is smart public policy because babies under one year of age are unlikely to benefit at all from formal group care and it's also the most expensive form of care during a child's highest dependency. Outsourcing care of babies is inefficient and estimated to cost two to three times more than the cost of a place for older children.

In 'universal' schemes, children at around three years of age begin to receive free or heavily subsidised part-time or full-time preschool. Preschool hours in many universal systems are also much shorter than our long daycare hours, which is another reason their childcare is cheaper. The preschool days are often no longer than 9am to 4pm, with a shorter working day for parents to accommodate the care of their children.

In Australia, we also have the unique problem of living on a very large island – 17 times the size of Iceland. Low and unevenly distributed population densities make the delivery of any universal system a constant struggle across transport, healthcare, and many other public services. Truly universal childcare will mean subsidising innovative models of childcare delivery in rural and remote areas where centres tend to operate at an unavoidable loss. It will mean subsidising alternative care models for rural families, thereby enabling them to provide the care themselves or procure their own informal carers.

Universal childcare has become one of those buzzwords that ends up being regurgitated over and again until the people saying it no longer have a clear understanding of what it actually means. Equating universal childcare with a completely free essential service misinterprets the aim of a universal system, which is simply to ensure childcare is available to everyone within their means and to the degree that is necessary to elicit benefits for the children and the workforce. We need *equitable* access to childcare, not equal access. It is not a one-size-fits-all situation.

The lack of action on behalf of the Australian government in relation to for-profit childcare providers is unacceptable, especially considering the number of times this issue has been brought to the attention of government inquiries. Most recently, in 2023, the Australian Competition & Consumer Commission's (ACCC) interim report into childcare sent a clear message to the government – it's time to face the music on for-profit childcare[104,105]. After decades of turning early-childhood development into a profit-making exercise, then attempting to subsidise it, it's time to stop throwing good money after bad policy. A handful of people have made some serious coin out of children, struggling families, and the taxpayer but authors of the report argued the free market alone can no longer be entrusted with the care of our youngest citizens.

The report found that not-for-profit childcare outperforms for-profit centres because staff are generally paid more and have better job security. The turnover of educators is lower in not-for-profit centres resulting in more stable, continuous care for children and stronger attachments to carers. Fees for families are more affordable. Not-for-profits also accept more vulnerable, disabled, or high-needs children, and are more likely to service disadvantaged communities.

Where the for-profits shine is in their ability to make money and expand rapidly in high-demand areas. Profit margins were on average 3% greater at for-profit centres than not-for-profit centres, with the latter being more likely to operate with negligible profits or at a loss. For-profits were better at driving down running costs by taking fewer high-needs children and paying lower wages. The incompatibility of the act of care with turning a profit has seldom been laid out in a more stark or distressing way.

Internal documents provided by centres to the ACCC explicitly referenced how the Child Care Subsidy is used to maintain or increase profits. This confirms what many parents have long suspected – that fee increases are being used to skim the subsidy. The taxpayer is funding profit margins rather than the intended target of struggling families. The report found parents were less sensitive to price changes if the perceived quality of care was high, but it was ultimately fee increases causing lower-income families to stop using childcare altogether.

The ACCC found centres increasingly couldn't care less about the hourly rate cap and that it was largely ineffective as a form of price discipline. The hourly rate cap, where fees are only subsidised up to an hourly rate of $13.73, was intended to constrain fee increases by signalling to centres what constitutes 'high fees'.

The report recommends more aggressive market controls such as direct price regulation and supply-side subsidies, which favour not-for-profits. It was recommended the government take on a stewardship role of the sector to 'financially sustain provision without funding excessive profits', and in some instances run centres directly.

It's important to understand exactly how Australia became so deeply wedded to for-profit childcare so we can appreciate the magnitude of the work ahead of us. Australian preschools first emerged in the 1890s to educate children experiencing poverty during the depression[106]. Day nurseries for single mothers engaged in paid work also began opening around this time. These were government-funded facilities. Services grew slowly, were not widespread, and remained largely state funded until the Australian Child Care Act of 1972 legislated funding for childcare services that could meet set criteria for opening hours. Instead of using public funds to build childcare as a public service, public funds were used to jump start the for-profit sector and it was incredibly successful in achieving the expansion of private childcare provision. By the time the Keating Labor government introduced the first childcare subsidy in 1991, the delivery of childcare-for-profit was well under way.

So, while Norway and Sweden were busy ploughing public funds into building a childcare sector that remains largely not-for-profit to this day, the Australian government was busy commodifying childhood. We were open for business. Given female representation in government was extremely low during the 1970s and remained low with women representing only 26% of federal parliamentarians in 2002, the architects of the Australian childcare sector we know today were predominantly male, had little experience of the day-to-day demands of care work, and lacked understanding of the intricacies of early-childhood development.

There was a genuine input from women wanting more choice, but the foundations of childcare delivery in Australia were largely built on business and economics rather than the wellbeing of women, children, and families. On the other hand, childcare sectors were in their infancy all around the world so there was little evidence of the poorer quality of for-profit childcare, how those systems might fail and potential problems that could arise. They could see a need for childcare services, but didn't value care and early childhood enough to include it as a public service.

It's also evidence of this idea that caring for children is so effortless and easy that anyone can do it. It's an insult to mothers everywhere that governments assumed you could commodify and easily replace a mother's work and care. And that work would be done cheaply with little government investment.

Australia deliberately assumed low-interference policies in the belief that competition among childcare providers would result in higher quality and downward pressure on prices. These architects did not foresee demand so strong that suppliers could practically name their price. They didn't foresee the development of a captive market that would be unable to afford housing on a single income and have no choice but to accept poor-quality care.

Underpinning our early development of the childcare sector

and still evident today is a reluctance to acknowledge the concept of wider society sharing the cost of raising children. As a result, Australia's investment in early childhood remains well below the OECD average. Where other nations accept a collective social responsibility for the public good that is the future generation of taxpayers, Australian policy continues to be influenced by individualism.

Even as serious cracks in the childcare sector began to appear at the turn of the millennium, the bipartisan failure of successive governments and their inability to act, continued. Perhaps the reason for our unwillingness to act sooner is the knowledge that the corporatisation and privatisation of childcare is notoriously difficult to undo. New Zealand is stuck in a similar bind. It's a very real possibility that the horse has bolted for nations with childcare sectors built by private funds.

The ACCC report showed there are bureaucrats who are brave enough to admit the folly of our approach to childcare and attempt to make it right. The questions that remain are: how much longer can government condone the prioritisation of profits over the wellbeing of children? How much can we spend on improving childcare centres before it becomes cheaper to subsidise parental care?

The best care and support, obviously, is that which isn't motivated by profits. The data shows this, but it also seems obvious that people with a genuine interest in our wellbeing, a shared history or a life-long investment in our wellbeing would provide the best care. Ultimately, in situations where care and education is delivered to turn a profit, the quality of the care has to compete with the ability of the business to make a profit.

Aside from the business model, our childcare sector faces an uphill battle in regulating centres.

In 2023, Australian childcare operators told the Independent

Pricing and Regulation Tribunal (IPART) that they are not price gouging but simply passing on the expense of caring for babies and children. Parents are 'our only lever that we have', as Broken Bay Catholic Care service put it to the IPART hearings.

The IPART investigation and hearings occurred in the lead up to a $4.1 billion childcare subsidy (CCS) increase. Childcare centres already appeared to be pre-emptively increasing fees ahead of this rise, continuing a price-rise trajectory up to five times faster than the rate of inflation in some areas. With no apparent significant increase in wages for educators in recent years, it begged the question – what are the relentless fee increases paying for?

The NSW Australian Childcare Alliance (ACA)—a peak body largely representative of the for-profit childcare sector—pointed the finger at regulatory burdens. In its submission to IPART it described how the National Quality Framework document has ballooned from 11 to 648 pages since its implementation in 2011. The ACA says the expense of compliance is prohibitive and that paperwork overload leads to burnout in educators and high turnover industry wide.

While this may explain part of the fee increases, regulation which ensures quality isn't an area we can cut costs when it comes to caring for children. The quality framework may be expensive to implement, and financially unviable in some cases but it has, at least on paper, led to an overall increase in quality of childcare centres. The tension between price and quality cuts to the heart of the issue when it comes to outsourcing the care of babies and young children – people expect quality care but they don't want to pay for it. Or they simply cannot afford it. This is where delivering acts of care on an industrial scale gets messy.

Childcare operators who gave evidence argued that regulations were critical to achieving high-quality care but said businesses would need to be subsidised by the government to avoid situations where providers were forced to cut costs and compromise care quality in order to remain viable. On the one hand, many operators are crying poor, on the other hand profits from childcare are flowing. What for-profit operators really mean is they can't pay for the price of regulation while also delivering fat profits to shareholders.

Interestingly, operators also argued the problem lay in the expectation that care should be cheap, arguing for the need to better educate parents on why quality care is so expensive.

It's not just the hefty price tag on quality care that's the problem, it's the enforcement of standards. Whether the quality ratings are actually worth the paper they are written on was another issue raised in evidence. Data from the Australian Children's Education & Care Quality Authority (ACECQA), the national regulatory body, shows many centres have not been assessed in the last five years. Given the average length of service of an educator at any one centre is 3.6 years, there is time for an entire turnover of staff between assessments at this rate. Families choosing centres today may be basing that decision on a five-year-old assessment with different staff at the helm. The government-funded regulatory body appears to need more money to properly enforce the 'high-quality' care politicians frequently talk about delivering.

Another explanation for the fee increases put forward in evidence was the rapid expansion of the for-profit childcare sector. 'Subsidies are funding profit as well as programming', the Community Early Learning Association writes in its submission. This is one point childcare sector representatives were not as forthcoming on in any of the three childcare-pricing inquiries held in Australia in recent years. One might even question whether the government really wants to know how much of the childcare subsidies end up in the pockets of big business owners and how to structure subsidies to prevent this.

The for-profit childcare sector has experienced rapid expansion in line with the rapid growth of subsidies, growing 30% since 2015.

Representatives of the broader childcare sector also claimed the large, for-profit childcare franchises were driving high-quality community-owned and not-for-profit centres out of the market, with the not-for-profit sector shrinking by 8% since 2015.

Organisations also reported that childcare was more expensive than ever due to increased behavioural issues in children. They say they have to have more staff, better staff, and higher-paid staff to manage the difficult behaviours emerging.

As I mentioned at the beginning of this chapter, Australia has been held up for over a decade as an international example of how *not* to structure a childcare sector. One of Australia's leading researchers, Professor Deborah Brennan, co-authored a Canadian research paper that described Australia's move away from non-profit childcare services as a 'spectacular public policy disaster'[107] and that increasing reliance on privatised childcare has had 'devastating consequences' for families.

The final difficulty arising in attempts to ensure childcare centres meet the needs of children and the families they service is understanding what practices actually result in great care. Quality is the holy grail of childcare, a caveat in any study that claims to find positive outcomes, but notoriously difficult to pin down and reproduce. Anecdotally and in research, we have both an inadequate understanding of what reliably results in quality care, how to measure the effectiveness, and how to consistently deliver that at scale. When researchers land on positive results in one setting or another, they often have great difficulty distilling the results to find the actual source of the benefit so that it may be replicated.

There are some clear quality indicators including high ratios of carers to children, low staff turnover, and warm, sequential interactions with children throughout the day. In relation to ratios, the regulations in Australia limit one caregiver to a maximum of four children under two years old, while the international recommendation is three children under two per caregiver, and many experts recommend just one or two babies per caregiver.

But even in ideal conditions some negative outcomes persist. As American psychoanalyst Sally Provence said in relation to a Yale University Childcare Pilot Program she observed for several years: "Group care, even under the best circumstances, is stressful for very young children ... the child from one to three is not by nature a highly suitable member of a large group."

We can pay carers more, we can select them for warmth in their demeanour, we can train them for years in sequential interactions and how to best interact with children but there is a limit to what a carer can achieve without accumulating significant amounts of on-the-ground experience with children and cultivating relationships based on secure attachment with each individual child they care for. As Anne Manne describes extensively in her book *Motherhood*, perhaps this difficulty in obtaining the high-quality care most likely to yield better outcomes is because it's often not characteristics of the care but the person who gives it. 'Right at the centre is the idea of irreplaceability, that a baby's love and attachment to their mother is an anti-commodity relationship. The thought that there is a fundamental particularity to love haunts, I think, all those who are never quite satisfied by the "quality care" arguments.'

Manne argues that synthesising the conditions that lead to quality care at scale is something of an impossibility. 'An attachment to a mother or father or substitute caregiver doesn't occur overnight,' she writes in her book. 'It takes many months as a baby's attachment behaviour is increasingly organised around their mother or a few special caregivers. A baby cannot simply flick a switch and "bond" conveniently with someone new. An attachment relationship is earned – it is the sensitivity and attentiveness of responding to a baby's signals that promotes a strong attachment.'

Carers must also be enabled to work under conditions that

allow them to devote the time and attention necessary to be able to develop the relationship and then deliver the quality care that would result. Even if a healthy attachment should somehow form between a carer in a childcare centre and a child under their care, the time constraints can make sequential interactions and a moment of genuine warmth or expressiveness difficult to achieve.

We begin to see that creating the ideal childcare conditions may cost more than lengthy, well-supported, gender-equitable paid parental leave. Hungarian sociologist Julia Szalai calculated that, largely due to higher infection rates in group care, the annual cost per child of parental leave was actually one third of the cost of running public daycare facilities[108].

Oxford Professor of Education Ted Melhuish told Manne, 'for the first 18 months to two years of life, the cost of good-quality care is potentially very high, and is comparable in cost to paid parental leave for two years ... To improve the responsiveness of group care requires maintaining very high staff-infant ratios and keeping staff turnover down to an absolute minimum: both are very expensive.' We also touched on this briefly in Chapter 6 when looking at calculations on the cost of poorer infant nutrition and negative health outcomes related to this as a result of earlier breastfeeding-cessation rates.

Childcare has served a purpose, it has shown us the potential of women across the paid and unpaid spectrum of economic contribution, but there are limits to what it can achieve for society going forward. We have to be realistic about the ability of centre-based childcare to meet infant needs – we can't magic childcare centres into something they are not and potentially can never be. We must be honest with ourselves if we are serious about at least improving childcare as an institution. For-profit dominance and quality issues cannot be ignored any longer.

In the words of American Anthropologist Sarah Blaffer Hrdy,

"Denial of infant needs runs like an invisible and insidious countercurrent through publications purporting to correct the 'river of mother-blame' coursing through our society ... what a relief to deep six the whole attachment enterprise and replace it with a new superstition about innately flexible and resilient ready-formed personalities wanting to emerge, for whom 'good-enough' care suffices in a world where it is considered crass to ask anyone to define what 'good enough' means."

At the time of going to print in Australia, the New South Wales Government had commenced an inquiry into the childcare system following a series of distressing reports of poor conditions and abuse occurring in childcare centres.

CHAPTER TWELVE

Rebuilding the Village

For daycare to become a truly effective village substitute it is imperative that measures are put in place to slow the turnover of staff and improve stability of relationships that families and children form with carers. When parents and children talk about feeling a deep sense of fondness for carers that have helped support and care for them over the years, when children grow up and can remember the names of preschool teachers or their carers, we can be confident that daycare and preschool have become an effective part of the village.

For daycare to be a legitimate part of a parent's village they must feel confident and comfortable with their decision, otherwise it can create an even more stressful situation where both mothers and children experience separation anxiety. Villages typically still facilitate proximity between children and parents. Modern applications of this could include increased opportunities for parents to engage in the care setting their child attends or have access to care settings on site. Fee models that charge hourly and only if a child attends could allow parents to be more flexible with spending time with their children if and when the opportunity arises.

Providing children with daycare within their local community helps strengthen their sense of belonging rather than having to make lengthy commutes to different towns or suburbs. Implementing long drop-offs and transitional programs for parents and children who are familiarising themselves with the daycare or preschool setting could also help develop trust and confidence. Allowing parents on site in a volunteer capacity can better integrate early-learning settings into villages as a whole.

Anthropologist Sarah Blaffer Hrdy describes the village-like, attachment-orientated daycare facility she used[109]. "The best place I found was the Harvard Yard Daycare Centre, whose program was designed by Berry Brazelton and other paediatricians heavily influenced by Bowlby ... These paediatricians, identified by the critics of attachment theory as special enemies of working mothers, were among those who made it possible for me to continue to work part-time even while my children were infants. A condition of leaving the baby there was volunteering to work in the nursery, so that in addition to the very permanent staff... there was a fluctuating contingent of family members in a tiny village-like setting, with a high ratio of adults to infants."

An Australian example of childcare designed to allow mothers and babies access to each other is the Sydney based Co-work Creche[110]. The site has a childcare space, play areas, communal kitchen and fully-equipped workspaces. There are an increasing number of on-site childcare centres in corporate work settings and, even, as one woman I spoke to explained – a tolerance of small children on site in some capacities. In a village setting, children and paid work aren't necessarily completely mutually exclusive ideas.

In rural areas where access to childcare is poor and, historically, we certainly see many examples of children being incorporated into our day-to-day work lives, whether that be in small or large capacities. It is surprising what happens when removing children from our paid work sphere is no longer an option – out of necessity many novel arrangements arise.

The tolerance of children in public or work settings is much lower, for the most part, simply because we have a heavy reliance on childcare centres and less experience of what it is like to live outside of that model. For some occupations and work settings, children would be a hazard at worst and impractical at best, but this doesn't negate the idea that there would be many scenarios where the presence of babies, at least, can and should be more widely accepted.

For daycare to more closely emulate a village setting, the workforce must be stabilised. Improved educator pay and working conditions is key in reducing turnover so that carers have more time to form quality attachments with the children they care for and become entrenched in a community even outside their workplace. Also, so that if a secure attachment is formed with a caregiver that person will likely remain a part of the child's life at least prior to starting school.

There are obvious limitations of any human being to simultaneously respond to a number of different children, particularly at unreasonable and demanding developmental stages, all day long or to maintain a parent-like investment in a child that is not their own. Increased supports for carers including volunteer parents or the ability to 'tap out' or tag team with other staff members can, in part, help reduce the stress inherent in the job.

It's worth noting that this conundrum—the trade-off between quality care more closely resembling a village setting and the economy achieved by having the least number of working-age adults as possible in charge of the greatest number of children—is not a design flaw of childcare, it is a built-in feature of group-care scenarios. The more children one adult can care for, the more working-age adults are freed up to engage in other 'more valuable' work, make supposedly more important contributions or return to higher-paid jobs. The pressures of group care that may be unfavourable in a developmental sense are also the most profitable and somewhat unavoidable when delivered at scale, but they can be alleviated through improving child-to-educator ratios.

At the seat of changing the way we deliver centre-based childcare, is changing our expectations, which have been hijacked by the commercialisation process. Because we have had the option of daycare centres that open from 6am to 6pm and require no parent input, societies quickly became accustomed to this delivery of care. Our work patterns changed because of this availability of not having our children in our care for vast, uninterrupted periods during the day. Realistic and beneficial childcare may involve parent interactions throughout the day, shorter hours, parent investment of time – all features that might present costs and inefficiencies to current business models. Features that might seem incompatible with working patterns which, as we have discussed, are presently unsustainable in both an economic and a health and wellbeing sense.

In order for daycares and preschools to function as a reasonable village substitute, they must not be overcrowded and under financial strain. In a counterintuitive sense, taking pressure off the daycare sector more broadly, contracting the industry, is conducive to allowing it to function more effectively as a support pillar. Continuous expansion beyond capacity—spreading the resources of the childcare sector too thin—is setting ourselves up to fail.

In this sense, how we build a village outside of childcare will determine how well childcare can function as a paid service. How well supported families are in their home life will determine how high-needs their children are in institutional settings and how much they must utilise services.

When we depopulate the village outside of paid help or paid work, families struggle regardless of how good their access to childcare. Once we have fewer people in the village to rely on, we outsource increasing amounts of labour or help, then we need more money to pay for the increased paid help, products and assistance, so we have to vacate the village to engage in paid work. The people who remain cannot then help us in a dynamic where, due to our paid work commitments, we would be unable to reciprocate.

Villages and the 'in kind' contributions they rely on don't work when it's only a handful of people operating outside the formal economy. The difficulty of creating a village is that it must reach critical mass to operate effectively. You need a whole group of people to collectively agree to commit to an amount of volunteer contribution or unpaid labour, which then enables the village to pool resources that may be shared and drawn on in time of need.

With numbers comes diversity of skill sets and a greater ability to get a variety of jobs done. Depopulation of our informal villages has occurred through later retirement ages, driving mothers back to work from earlier and earlier ages, and a general culture that values overwork, material possessions, and professional success over connection, community, and common decency. Villages are starved of people to contribute, who understand how it works, which leaves them weak and dysfunctional.

The market economy has largely filled the void left by the absence of village and informal help. Committees and volunteer-led organisations everywhere are dying, outsourcing tasks to the market or remunerating positions. You can pay someone to be at the birth of your child, a doula, and you can even pay someone to help you in the weeks after the birth – a postpartum doula. The examples of this commercialisation of what previously were deeply personal community functions are endless but quite necessary, and often very effective as a substitute paid village.

Still, caution must be exercised with how much we let commerce take over informal, interpersonal relations. Something is lost when money changes hands – that person is now there, at least in part, because you paid them, not because they care about you as a person. Conversely, paying someone for their services removes part of the social contract for the payer. You are less obligated to be a nice person precisely because you paid them and you expect them to do their job either way.

The interaction is contingent on payment rather than preserving the relationship. If you don't like them or the job they do, you can simply cut ties.

In 2000, researchers from the University of California found that introducing late fines at a daycare centre increased the instances of late pick-ups rather than deterring them. Why? Because when parents knew staff were staying late on their behalf without recompense they felt guilty and were much more keen to prevent the situation occurring. But once they knew they could pay to be late, the social contract was negated.

A lot of people claim to want a village but I don't think they realise that this involves input and effort, forgoing an amount of leisure time and possibly even lost income. It's not a one-way street. Time is money and many people would say they simply could not afford to contribute their time. It's also undeniably about our priorities. We can't strive for something we don't really understand, something we haven't experienced the benefits of, and when money is the only language we speak.

David Attenborough famously said about nature, "No one will protect what they don't care about; and no one will care about what they have never experienced." I think the same applies for community and the village. It is a learned skill. You have to know what is being lost to defend it.

Five years ago we drove our growing family[iii] 12 hours south for a higher-paying job. We didn't know a soul. I had to use Google Maps to find my way to anywhere. I was pregnant and had two kids under four. We weren't to know it then but the community we moved to was about to show us the meaning of 'having a village'.

I thought I knew what community was about, but I'd grown up with my entire family in the same postcode. I took that sense of belonging and unwavering support for granted. My family was my community. I relied on them and, particularly as a younger person, offered not much in return. I enjoyed the fruits of community but did none of the labour.

Then I left the nest for school, university, and my first job. By that stage, I was young, child-free, had my own money and work friends. A kind of self-reliance set in and, other than social events, I had little need for community in a practical sense. I could do it myself or pay someone for help. This is how I never got around to learning how the village actually works.

Roughly three months after we moved across the state, COVID lockdowns began. By then, I had three children under six and spent long hours without any adult company at our home. We lived on a farm out of town and the isolation crept up on me. Things started to go downhill. Not long after that, my sister died.

The first thing that happens in a true village is people don't give vague offers for help – they know what needs to be done and they do it. 'Is it OK if we come on Wednesday to prune the roses?' the text message read. I remember being mildly shocked that someone would volunteer themselves in this way. There is a long list of great acts of kindness shown to us during that terrible time but for some reason, I will never forget the roses. The way people just materialised to help us, who weren't family and were not being paid, was foreign to me.

The benefits of a village were shown to me by the kindness of others, and over time I gradually realised how much you get in return. It was only by learning from others how rewarding, helpful, and necessary the village is. I also had the benefit of having a mother who volunteered and contributed, so I had a rough idea of what contributing meant. Many people never find themselves in a well-established community that can take them under their wing and show them the ropes. Some people are never shown one of the last remaining vestiges of humanity outside the market economy.

Little by little our unpaid village appeared and we put our roots down. We joined a few committees, a couple more sports teams, and a book club to which I am wholly devoted. My neighbour teaches me Pilates free of charge. We contribute our time and effort, I feel more comfortable accepting help, though I still compulsively try to pay people for it. The capitalist in me is constantly at war with the socialist.

When I tore almost every useful ligament in my knee, I still struggled to accept the help, people arriving at my door ready to clean or bearing pre-cooked meals. I'm eternally grateful for the help, but my social conditioning and my yearning for an exactness in the transaction means I compulsively try to pay people.

Having a village also involves social interactions that can be awkward verging on painful, and dealing with people who aren't your cup of tea. People who form the village aren't robots, they are diverse and they aren't as reliable as an employee. Having a village will require more social interaction than a lot of people are willing to give. Deep down, people don't want or can't manage the unreliability of dealing with those in an informal setting. A village can be inconvenient.

Due to the loss of skills and people in informal settings, policy will be a crucial catalyst in rebuilding parts of the village that can help children thrive. Conditions conducive to informal villages can be artificially created before the village dynamics start to emerge in an organic sense.

As an example, extensive Paid and Unpaid Parental Leave schemes can repopulate parts of the village outside of paid work, which in turn strengthens 'the village' through sheer numbers – by enabling more parents to remain outside the paid workforce and in caregiving roles for longer periods. Short parental leave periods often mean parents don't have enough time to become established in their communities outside of work in social, hobby, or volunteer capacities. Short-term deadlines to return to work add inherent pressure even while on parental leave and can mean people don't commit to long-term community projects.

Village-building strategies must also be implemented in a town planning sense to keep communities better connected geographically. Clever town planning can allow for both privacy at home but then once in public can encourage incidental interactions, the chance to physically be near other people, see them and talk to them. It can also lead to less insulated modes of travel. Where cars are a physical barrier between us and the world around us, walking paths, cycling paths, and effective public transport systems bring us physically together and allow more incidental interactions.

A policy like the Home Care Allowance, in place in several Nordic countries and discussed in Chapter 9, provides support for families who opt out of daycare for under threes and support payments at birth for those who may not meet the work test for a variety of reasons, such as having children close together or choosing to assume caregiving responsibilities in a longer term capacity. Legitimising the community of unpaid carers through income support is a way of strengthening the village because unpaid carers are more able to form support networks among each other. When we are supported we feel more able to help others, volunteer, socialise, and build community.

Rebuilding the village requires an understanding of the value of that social infrastructure and the value of unpaid contributions. But it also requires policies that support and legitimise these unpaid contributions.

CHAPTER THIRTEEN

Reclaiming Care from Capitalism

"One! Two! Fee!" This is how I remember my two-year-old son counting the chicken's eggs. He learned about the world every time we ventured out the door. Every time we sang a song, visited a neighbour, paid for groceries, and every time somebody engaged him in conversation – his little sponge of a brain soaked it up. By then I had realised that children can be raised, socialised, and receive their 'early childhood education' through the rich, mundane or stimulating experiences that make up our everyday lives. That caring functions need not be sanitised, regulated, and centred in the market economy. I didn't have to buy my son an early childhood. Care can be self-organised and self-governed in a way that meets human need effectively.

I remember distinctly the first time another mother offered to mind my kids while I helped out with a Parents and Carers Committee project after school one afternoon. I had thought my children would play happily in the playground while I volunteered but it turned out they had other ideas and she picked up on this. She simply saw a need. It never occurred to me that someone else in the community might be able to have them. Less still, that the kids would actually enjoy it and that the favour would be offered freely.

"Okay, well... I guess if you're sure? Are you sure that would be okay? Please don't feel like you have to." I stumbled on and on. This was unfamiliar territory, my mind was in overdrive, but eventually I ran out of excuses not to accept the offer. She is a lovely friend, I knew the family and the kids got along famously. It now stands out as a point in time where my unlearning of individualism and capitalism played out for all to see. Why would I have never thought to offer that? This seemed too easy. What was the catch?

Even though I had already, in a sense, largely realised commercial-care options did not meet my family's needs, I was still in the process of discovering the myriad ways a village could fill the void daycare leaves. I was in the process of shedding my individualist skin and returning care to 'the commons'. In 2016 I began enlisting the help of family and friends, brought my children to jobs and eventually hired a nanny one day a week.

I had never heard of 'care-commoning' until a PhD student, Sara Caspiani, organised a Zoom meeting to discuss the concept late in 2024. Even now, if you search it online, the information is not widely available and comes from small, grassroots organisations. It's important to understand that commoning care is a cumulative experience – it doesn't happen overnight, it must be built and it initially requires a concerted effort to seek alternatives. It also requires certain preconditions like fragments of existing community-support functions or at least the potential for them to grow. Had I not initially sought alternatives to centre-based childcare settings, had others not kindly shown me the way at times, the arrangements I eventually had access to might never have eventuated and been able to flourish. The opportunities for creative solutions are stifled by blind reliance on and acceptance of commercial settings for early childhoods.

What makes care-commoning distinct from commercial childcare settings is that there is often no money exchanged. Care functions may be performed as a trade; for example, minding another's children on a casual, semi-regular or regular basis in exchange for childminding help in return. Care functions are also sometimes provided for altruistic reasons without expectation of any kind of recompense. This is due to a sense of duty to the child; for example, a grandparent or relative, and being invested in the child's wellbeing. Care work might also be performed with the intent of preserving a relationship we feel is intrinsically valuable, particularly for emotional or social support. At times, it is a combination of all three – we help because we need help in return, we feel a sense of duty or obligation to people we care about and to the children, and we want to preserve the relationship.

If money does exchange hands in the commons there are added layers where that service is still valued intrinsically and there is a desire to preserve a pre-existing relationship with that person. Paid agreements are often entered into with more informal contractual arrangements and carried out by small and independent providers. For example, you have a friend or relative in your community and decide to pay them for the care work they provide. This might be in the event that there is no practical in-kind trade able to be agreed upon.

Commoning 'arises from the realisation that neither markets nor states can fully address the complex social and environmental challenges we currently face', as articulated by a group in the UK called Incommons.

Care-commoning recognises that care work is best done as shared work in common spaces but rejects the commercialisation of this process. Commoning is 'generative of relationships' – a kind of antithesis to the capitalist systems that are contingent on monetary transactions and isolating people so they rely more on outsourcing functions that may have previously existed outside the market economy.

Commoning of early-childhood care sometimes occurs at larger scale out of necessity in areas where centre care is difficult to access. This phenomenon was observed empirically in Spain and Italy as a result of the Global Financial Crisis. Southern European cities like Barcelona and Naples were hard hit by austerity measures and many childcare centres closed or became unaffordable. I might add that these regions were not as culturally invested in commercial daycare as we are in places like Australia and New Zealand. The family and community cultures in Italy and Spain, the acceptance of children in public spaces and tolerance of them is much higher. In her paper *Childcare Commons*, Manuela Zechner summarises the way childcare commons have grown in Naples.

'In a nutshell, *grupos de crianza compartida* are groups of parents allied with educators, who run self-organized nurseries, mostly in rented shopfront spaces. If they are initiated by parents, they form a shared vision and define shared needs, usually find a trained educator to accompany them (an *acompañante*), constitute an association, find a space, and begin a routine of daily childcare. If they start from educators, the process is similar but group formation is often slower and facilitated more strongly by educators. Groups might shift from being more parent-run to being more teacher-run—and vice versa—and involve different degrees of sharing the work of childcare as well as organization. What defines them is the notion of childcare as a common matter that requires sharing work—as care work and/or organizational work—and building community[112].

'The more organically, carefully and slowly these groups can constitute themselves—the less market-like—the more likely they are to thrive, by building good collective process, debating doubts and tensions, getting information, taking legal and administrative steps in time, getting the children used to the educators slowly, finding and equipping a space, and reaching out to the neighbourhood to fill places and gather support, dealing with people leaving and joining the project. *Grupos de crianza* lead parents, educators and children to work together and constitute a strong care network as well as neighbourhood *tribú*, focusing care both inward (*tribu*) and outward (neighbourhood). They recognize that modern urban parenting is an individualizing and precarious matter that requires new support structures.'

Care-commoning practices in Naples were also observed in similar circumstances and explored as a potential solution to the social reproduction crisis that also plagues these areas[113]. If care in the commons was better able to meet the needs of families, improving the experience and affordability of having children, then governments could use this as a demographic lever that offered economic relief in the form of increasing birth rates. What was lost in GDP could be regained in human capital.

Some researchers have even positioned commoning care as a potential solution to the limitations of endless economic growth in the context of finite planetary resources, which has resulted in productivity stagnation and environmental pressures. If care provided in the commons was better able to meet human need (emotionally and physiologically), improved public health outcomes and created economic efficiencies (for example, by lowering public health costs or eliminating or reducing work commutes) all while shoring up the production of human capital and stabilising social reproduction, shouldn't it be enlisted as a strategy to stabilise economies around the world? These care-commoning practices have revealed themselves as a way of decreasing reliance on consumption, lowering the market activity of a sector while still maintaining important underlying economic functions like a stable future labour force. It offers a kind of soft landing if we are to implement ways to move towards steady states that are still able to service the needs of the population.

Returning care to the commons happens in various forms all over the world. We see similar responses in rural and remote areas in Australia. In my local community, far enough from the nearest daycare centre to make it an impractical care solution, the accumulation of enough families with children of similar ages triggered effective communal caregiving arrangements. We mind each other's children in exchange for childcare in return. While it is mostly an arrangement born out of necessity, it is a beneficial, flexible, community-based arrangement that may never have formed had all these children been in a childcare centre. This arrangement might also occur where parents don't see centre-based care as an option for their child due to complex needs or personal preferences.

Commercial childcare is a classic example of inappropriate city solutions being foisted upon regional families despite being largely unworkable in many rural contexts. People in the bush have been quietly chipping away to solve this problem themselves. In some particularly remote areas it is big business that has been able to capitalise on benefits of the commons, such as pre-existing community ties, spaces and interpersonal relationships, by pioneering a kind of hybrid commons – commercial care arrangement.

In 2015, BHP commenced a pilot program that saw existing houses—often company houses—transformed into Family Day Care facilities run by the spouses of employees. The iron-ore company's grants program allowed local people to gain necessary qualifications and fit out their homes to fill a vital need in close proximity to other remote families. The program was so successful that it continues a decade on in regional communities all over Australia and services families outside the companies.

While, in the end, these programs can become a commercial transaction, they are essentially piloted and governed by the local community. Other industries such as agriculture and defence are seeking to emulate the model of cultivating Family Day Care providers to support their own respective labour forces. In 2022, GrainGrowers entered the planning stages of a pilot program with Family Day Care Australia (FDCA). In its most recent annual report the FDCA said the interest from industry would continue to grow. 'The project represents clear evidence for the appetite of industry operating in regional areas of need … This program … will pave the way for other projects with BHP and other regional pilots moving forward.'

The model of family daycare collaborating with industry works because it's an efficient formalisation of tried-and-true informal childcare models that have been in use since humans started roaming the planet. A nearby mother or grandmother who is willing and able starts minding children from other families in exchange for payment in kind – goods or child minding in return. The BHP program is a way of regulating a communal-care arrangement and rendering it eligible for the childcare subsidy.

The utilisation of existing facilities and people already based in these communities is a no brainer; the commoning of care or at least elements of this concept is a legitimate solution, so why has it been so badly overlooked? Why does it repeatedly fail to enter the discourse around early years and childcare deserts? One theory is that this approach eliminates the need for large, for-profit childcare franchises to set up centres in regional areas and take advantage of an enormous level of government subsidies that would be required to make these facilities financially viable. Presumably, childcare lobby groups do not want their members circumvented in this way.

Another possible theory is that the centre-based childcare model is just so dominant in the early-years narrative that people now fail to see solutions beyond it. Centre-based care is an absolute cultural monopoly that has been normalised to the point that people are now mildly suspicious of alternative or informal care arrangements. A blinkered view of the early years has evolved where many in policy-making settings view centre-based care as the only appropriate model of care worth funding, regardless of whether it helps families in a diverse range of settings.

Most rural families are solving the childcare problem by doing it themselves, recruiting the help of family and friends, or hiring help privately. They curate their own unsubsidised 'childcare packages' with the resources they have. I have a nanny one day per week, neighbours who can lend a hand, grandparent help, and a husband in relatively flexible paid employment – this commoning of care is the sole reason I am able to write this book and remain attached to the labour force in some capacity. They enrich the children's lives enormously, yet they are absent in early-years policy discussions.

Parents in rural areas also deal with isolation that is alleviated by this support and social contact. On days when I know help is on the way, I can feel the weight lift. We weren't meant to do this alone. We are using the only options available to us, in the same way that city-based families use the options available to them. The only difference being that city-based families are subsidised for their choices whereas rural families are not.

If politicians and childcare advocates were serious about supporting young families in the bush, there are myriad solutions they could be implementing. They could start with an expansion of the In Home Care program, a program where care is provided in the home for families for whom centre-based care is not available or appropriate. In addition, broadening of the eligibility criteria for this program would deliver immediate support to thousands of families in rural areas. At present, the program has the capacity to support 3000 places, a fraction of the estimated nine million Australians currently living in areas with insufficient childcare availability.

Better resourcing of this program would be critical as many families, including ourselves, have been approved to receive the subsidy to use an In Home Care provider but have been unable to find one available. Our nanny is a qualified teacher's aide and a veritable gift to humanity, yet astonishingly, does not meet the criteria that would allow her to be subsidised under the In Home Care program. We also found the projected costs per day of approved carers delivered through IHC were more expensive than hiring an unsubsidised nanny ourselves.

A Nanny Pilot program was trialled by the Morrison Liberal Government in 2016 to address the above shortfalls in the In Home Care Program and allow rural families to source their own carers as long as they had a Working With Children Check, were over 18, and held a current first aid certificate. The program, though by no means perfect in its delivery, was ultimately dropped amid concerns over quality control. This seems ludicrous given the fact that most rural families who hire help privately will do it anyway, and most grandparents and parents do not hold formal early-childhood care and education qualifications. The care is often carried out with a parent on site and able to monitor quality of care with their own eyes.

A subsidy or support to engage grandparent carers who are picking up the slack created by the market failures of corporate childcare would also go some way to supporting rural families, or any families for whom centre-based daycare wasn't a preference. Grandparent care is also often a kind of bridge for toddlers or children transitioning from parent care to formal care arrangements. In 2015, National Seniors Australia highlighted the increasing significance of grandparent carers and the need for policy to respond to this. Over half of the grandparents surveyed believed the government should offer some form of subsidy, even if only for costs incurred while caring for grandchildren such as transport. Grandparents remain the most popular model of outsourcing childcare for Australian families. Anecdotally, I think it's safe to say the kids like them too.

I attended a small mobile preschool in a tiny country town and it's something I have prioritised for my kids. That rural families travelling hundreds of kilometres to preschool each week aren't at least subsidised for travel costs is one of the most blatant gaps in early-years policy in the regions. In Norway, parents report high levels of satisfaction with using a similar model for young children who aren't in institutional care except they call them Open Kindergartens. Open Kindergartens often have maternal child health services on site as do some playgroups in Australia.

Governments have the potential to better utilise the commons as part of the early-years solutions. There is a need to investigate measures that support parents to optimise their children's development in the community when they have no other viable option or if this is their preference. Parent education materials as well as learning and development aids could be delivered to families in the bush or those who opt out of daycare. Carer payments could assist parents to deliver early-learning programs themselves. Where the population is sparse, where the distances are huge, and where the viability of for-profit group care is uncertain, support payments to parents themselves start to make more financial sense than a subsidy to outsource the care.

Some local councils throughout Australia still facilitate a system similar to the BHP model where members of the community are supported to operate a Family Day Care service. Although many councils have abandoned this practice, such as Albury City Council which stated, 'Increased regulatory, compliance and resourcing requirements have made it unviable for Albury City to continue to offer Family Day Care services into the future.' Some FDC council programs continue to be very successful. Fairfield City Council has one of the longest running Family Daycare Departments, which has assisted hundreds of carers over the years set up their own facility in their home. However, judging by the current trends the future of these council services seems uncertain.

If not for practical or logistical reasons, or the idea that community settings can more genuinely and effectively meet human needs, there is also a strong preference among parents for raising children in the commons. I interviewed two rural mothers a few years ago who articulated the realisation that centre-based care wasn't an option or a preference for them.

Karla Carruthers was coaching some of the most promising athletes in the bush in the final months of her pregnancy in 2021. She told the local swimming club and her students she would be back soon, but the arrival of her son changed everything. "I just assumed he would be fine to tag along and it would still all run smoothly," Karla explains. "I soon realised it was not that easy." As a swimming coach and personal trainer, Karla worked early-morning sessions and later afternoon shifts that went into the evening. "It's simply not doable with a baby at those times when they need you the most. I realised I would have to either put him in care or give up my job as a coach, which I loved."

The weeks turned to months in her new role as a mum and Karla felt her life was full looking after her son. She was comfortable with her decision and felt intensely grateful that she was able to afford to take time out of paid work to look after her baby. As a family, they made difficult financial decisions so they could afford to live on a single income, including her partner taking on more work hours.

The sacrifice 'working mothers' make and their extraordinary workload is widely recognised, their preference to engage in paid work is also respected, and rightly so, but the decision to contribute care—also an exhausting and worthy role—is often undervalued and under-supported. Karla has felt a sense of guilt, as though she is not contributing, which is then compounded by a sense of professional sacrifice. "It was very hard for me to give up something I really loved but at the same time I knew that the regret of not being home with my son watching him grow far outweighed the regret of not returning to work."

While Karla has placed great significance in her work caring for her son, she noticed others were uncomfortable with her decision to enter a long-term caring role. "I have felt extreme pressure from society to have someone else care for my son and still get asked when he is going to daycare," she says. "These years are so important and it's essential to me that I'm the one who is teaching him as he grows. The bond we share being together still breastfeeding at two years is so beautiful."

Mothers have been going through the shock of adjusting to the reality of having a baby since time immemorial, but in an increasingly isolating, work-centred and time-pressured society, modern mothers face unique challenges. The difficulties are often compounded for rural mothers who experience long travel times and poor access to subsidised childcare. Across the board, the transition to motherhood is complicated exponentially by the societal expectation to return to paid work.

In her book, *Motherhood*, Anne Manne writes of this tension, 'Work is the more powerful culture, creating a kind of cultural necessity to put work first.' She cites feminist Arlie Hochschild who argues, 'work is less often a simple economic fact than a complex cultural value. If in the early part of the century it was considered unfortunate that a woman had to work, it is now surprising when she doesn't.'

Felicity Bowen also surprised people in her decision to delay her return to paid work in order to care for her children on their family farm near Cassilis in New South Wales. "I felt like it was me doing something unnatural choosing to stay at home with my child and being there for her as she developed and navigated this new world," Felicity remembers. "I thought people felt like I had a poor work ethic and thoughts crept in about letting my family down financially. When my first child was about six months old, a lot of the mums from mother's group had returned to work. My daughter was still so tiny and dependant on me for stability, safety, security, and milk! I started getting the question about when I planned to return to work from a lot of well-intentioned friends and family."

Despite feeling isolated and undervalued, Felicity took two years' leave after the birth of her daughter, Cecilia. She returned to her teaching role one day a week before the arrival of her son, Wilfred, at which point the logistics of commuting 64 kilometres to town with kids felt unmanageable and unsustainable. Felicity could see that caring for her kids at home would be a more enriching experience and also meant they would be able to spend more time with their dad who works on the farm. "There are many opportunities for him to have smoko with the kids and for us to picnic on the farm where he may be sowing," Felicity explains. "The kids are able to participate in moving stock, conducting slow burns, woodchopping, planting trees, building fences and so forth."

Felicity's local town enjoys a not-for-profit mobile outreach program called Toybox that provides fortnightly parental support and educational activities for children in isolated areas. She also goes to public libraries for Storytime programs. "Having a connection to community and being able to talk through parental experiences with others makes being a stay-at-home parent a lot easier."

As someone who was heavily invested in her teaching career, Felicity still struggles at times with her new identity. It has been difficult to move away from the career she spent so much time and energy building. "I am a proud feminist but I feel at odds with feminist commentators that suggest stay-at-home-mums have been duped by the patriarchy into thinking that this is what they want. There seems to be a sense of internalised misogyny in the idea that the choice to be maternal is 'a lesser choice'. I feel my purpose in my family is valid and valuable, but often this is at odds with society's perspective and what is 'good for the economy'."

Mothers in full-time caregiving roles are further alienated by an inability to talk about their decision and challenges they experience for fear of offending mothers who have made different choices or been forced to return to work for financial reasons. The value of 'working mothers' in their increased paid contribution and professional gains is often referenced in social and political discourse; however, an attempt to illustrate the value of the unpaid care contribution is often seen as an attempt to shame mothers who return to paid work.

Felicity has felt unable to participate in conversations where other parents explain they returned to work because being a 'stay-at-home' parent is 'mind numbingly boring' or intellectually unsatisfying. "I often remain tight-lipped about my choice to stay at home for fear of offending those who want to engage in paid work," she explains. "I respect the choice of other parents, but I would also like to be afforded the same respect for doing what I think is in the best interests of my family too."

Lack of childcare was a factor in Felicity's decision to enter a full-time care-giving role, highlighting how many rural women still lack a sense of genuine choice in paid-work participation due to the existence of 'childcare deserts'. She was excited about securing a great part-time role only to find the child hours weren't available in her local area. "I do panic at times that dream opportunities come up while I'm in this caregiving period of my life, and they may not be available when I am ready to return to work, and also, I'll likely not be seen as employable when I have an extended period of absence from the workforce on my resume."

Felicity and Kara fit the definition of 'maternal feminists'. Anne Manne describes maternal feminists as 'more radical, seeking more profound structural change, than "equality as sameness" feminism, which seeks to accommodate women by minimising their family baggage.'

Taking a substantial amount of time away from the workforce in order to carry out unpaid care responsibilities often leaves women in a vulnerable financial position. Support for women to enter paid work is critical, but Felicity and Kara would like to see similar support for the vital work of unpaid carers.

"We need real and genuine recognition that unpaid care is a legitimate choice along with financial protections," Felicity says. "I've previously struggled with absorbing messages that my choice is 'lazy' and not valued by Australian society, but I am learning to shake this off. Women can try to 'have it all' but I would be running myself ragged if I tried, and I feel fulfilled providing the safe, healthy, stable, and stimulating homelife for my family."

CHAPTER FOURTEEN

The Money Problem

One of the most common arguments that arises when discussing the issue of both parents working increasingly long hours, and the impacts this has on children or parents, is that some families simply cannot afford to live on one income. There are legitimate financial challenges and macroeconomic conditions that increasingly require families to earn dual incomes. Housing price increases have outstripped inflation. Wage growth is still occurring but at a much slower rate than previous generations due to tighter labour market conditions and tighter profit margins. Pressure on natural resources and climate issues have tended to destabilise food production and increase the price of many goods, including food, electricity, gas, and fuel.

Rather than recognising how problematic it is that parents have *no choice* but to outsource many aspects of raising their children in order to survive financially, we commonly end up with a reductive, fatalistic, avoidant, and defeatist view of the issue which goes something like this: "Both parents have to work for reasons that are too big and complex to ever solve, therefore, let's stop attempting to find solutions to the fundamental problems and simply mask the symptoms. We shouldn't distress families by pointing out the drawbacks of the dual-income society they find themselves in if we can never change it."

This is flawed logic for one key reason – change isn't just possible, it is the only future we have. This is not a question of whether we move away from capitalistic growth systems that undermine our own ability to care for ourselves and reproduce, it's a question of when. Our hand will be forced eventually; we either start preparing now to soften the landing or we continue masking symptoms while the problem worsens.

My specialty is not economics, granted, but it doesn't take a fancy education to see the unacceptable suffering and damage that occurs in existing systems. There are many scholars and leaders who have devoted their lives to solving these fundamental economic problems. Herman Daly, Jason Hickel, Raworth to name a few, but most you and I have never heard of. Post-growth, steady-state, degrowth, ecological economics, bastardised capitalism—call it whatever you want—many economists have recognised the bare-faced stupidity of puritan capitalism and free markets that have set us on our current trajectory. They have developed countless ways to transition away from the failed growth economy we find ourselves in.

The steady-state arguments centre on setting production boundaries within limits of what we can safely produce while meeting human need. There are legitimate concerns that shrinking the economy will lead to even poorer living standards, less tax revenue to pay for public services, and breakdown of social cohesion as people compete for resources and jobs. Steady-state proponents frequently acknowledge this in their work, stating that transitioning to steady-state economies is a process that will take many decades and would need to be planned and executed meticulously. Arguably, trends like declining birthrates will shrink the economy anyway, but in an uncontrolled and rapid way that leads to even harsher declines in living standards. Stabilising now may mean we miss the highest peaks of boom times that growth economies promise (if we find new inputs), but it also means we avoid the crash.

If we don't address the fundamental problems with the way our economy is structured and the dual-income society that has emerged as a result, we are actually complicit in making the problem worse. Most families are no longer in a position where they have financial mobility, where they can change their financial situation by simply sending another labourer into the market, like we did when women entered the workforce. Most households have nothing left to give. Our financial instability and quality of life will get progressively worse if we attempt to keep throwing more labour and production into an economy that simply eats it up, grows to accommodate the growth, and then comes back for more. We simply have to change, and we can, but only if we make clear the irreducible problems growth economies and the dual-income society cause. Only if we take seriously, at the highest levels of decision making and leadership, the merit of economic research that points to stabilised economies and populations.

There are often attempts to argue that cost-of-living pressures haven't actually changed and that people have simply forgotten how to budget or they don't work hard enough. All sorts of equations and graphs have been trotted out to try to prove that the costs-of-living we encounter today are the same as 50 years ago after you account for inflation and indexation or other details. This argument has a simple purpose of placing responsibility for the economic challenges we face solely with the individual. People want to believe that it's simply a problem of human behaviour, which arguably can be altered, rather than systemic and entrenched functions of the economy.

My position on this is that we have enough data from legitimate sources to agree that cost-of-living pressures are higher for families today than they have ever been. Some of our financial problems are within our control and some are not. The Productivity Commission (PC) released a report in October 2024 that showed those born in the 1990s are the first cohort to miss out on substantially higher incomes than their predecessors. The PC traces lower income growth back to lower productivity, which can then be traced back to lower birth rates. The conclusions drawn by the PC were largely that due to slower population growth and demographics, we will not be able to continue to prop up economic growth with increasing labour force participation. This has been a lever available to us for the last three or four decades as women drastically increased their labour-force participation, and retirement ages blew out. But with increases in parent participation in the labour force now tapering off alongside growth in life expectancy, the PC now says growth in productivity will have to come from technological advances and finding efficiencies if we are to reduce financial pressures on families of the future.

Parents literally have fewer hours left to give to the labour market, with 25% of families with children under five already having both parents working full-time. There are signs we are reaching a plateau in retirement age, with over 55s representing 70% of the increase in labour force from 2019 to 2021, but that share of the increase fell back to 21.3% in the two years to 2023. The limits on human longevity, how functional our bodies and brains remain into old age, represent a factor in the economic slowdown.

In her book, *Two Income Trap*, Elizabeth Warren[114] argues that shaping society around a dual income becomes a trap for families and leaves them less financially secure than if they had a parent at home. After an initial period where dual-income families have increased financial security and increased disposable income, and as dual-incomes slowly become the norm, prices increase in response. Dual-income families outbid single-income families for houses in family-friendly areas and near good schools, so the pressure to transition to dual incomes increases until almost every family increases their earning power. The growth in family spending power, at least in part, fed inflation and growth in prices, ultimately negating the increase in earning power.

Families reach a ceiling in their earning power and find themselves back at square one, with no capacity to simply 'work more' and make more money to get ahead. Understandably, families who reach this point are angry and find themselves in an even more precarious financial situation than some single-income families. They sacrifice precious time with family and children, they sacrifice their health and wellbeing, their happiness, only to find the 'better life' was a mirage. They aren't really able to get ahead.

The other element of the trap is that couples delay having children, get used to six-figure lifestyles or whatever they earn as a DINK (Double Income No Kids), buy cars and homes based on this income, and then have children and realise they can't see them during business hours if they want to keep a roof over their heads.

While Warren's figures are debated and the exact level of the increase in cost-of-living pressures is hard to pin down, what is clear is that in a dual-income society the bankruptcy levels of middle- and middle-high income families in America increased dramatically. Warren pins most of the financial struggle to increases in mortgage payments and other long-term fixed costs. She argues for changes to bankruptcy laws, lending and credit regulation and increased government financial support for families so that they may still live in family-friendly areas and access good schools while also maintaining financial stability.

While increased government support will be critical to addressing the complex macroeconomic conditions we now face, legitimate financial struggles are not the entire story. Our spending patterns— what we spend our money on and how much we spend—have changed wildly since the 1970s. In a different book by the same name (*The Two Income Trap*), Suzanne Venker[115], also argues that we have become victims of a dual-income trap but that it is more a result of financial illiteracy, the inability to budget, and rampant overconsumption.

I think it's somewhere in the middle. We underestimated or failed to predict the extent to which the rapid rise of dual incomes would shape our economy. We also underestimate the scourge of overconsumption, the way advertising and social media constantly sabotage our ability to live within our means. How much more entitled we feel we are to items that were once considered a luxury. What appears to be 'not having a choice' is actually often an unwillingness to have less or live in a smaller home in a mediocre neighbourhood.

While we have moved to a society where class is less visible in some ways and opportunities are more equal, social media and home ownership chasms have served to make different levels of wealth much more visible. Which brings me to a phenomenon called 'relative deprivation'.

We all know comparison is the thief of joy, no doubt uttering this to ourselves as we rubberneck around the coastal real estate while on holiday, but the problem is that we are hardwired for social comparison[116]. The ability to compare ourselves to others and adjust is how we evolved as a species. For millennia, not 'going with the crowd' or not 'keeping up with the Joneses' placed us in mortal danger. We noticed the people with the fire and unless we had the wherewithal to emulate them, our line was quickly bred out. We evolved to be deeply attuned to those around us and how we compared. Researchers estimate that comparison dominates around 10% of all our thoughts on average.

Instead of emulating starting a fire or building wheels to transport things, we now try to emulate modern markers of progress or success – professional achievement and wealth. What exactly did they do to be able to afford that yacht? That school? Those clothes? Comparison can be an important motivating factor and helps us aspire to great achievements, but it becomes a problem when we lack social or financial mobility. Social comparison is depressing and demotivating if we are constantly exposed to material wealth or achievement that is unattainable; for example, fortunes underpinned by generational wealth or achievements underpinned by social privileges.

Increasing wealth inequality and stubborn social inequalities combined with a social media parallel universe where we are frequently exposed to extreme wealth or achievement, means social comparison is less the self-improvement tool it once was and instead breeds resentment. We can see the yacht, we know we want the yacht, but we can't simply learn how to get a yacht. We likely will never get a yacht and then we feel hard done by, even though according to Maslow, our needs are comfortably met and we are on a lovely holiday at the beach. The more people start getting yachts, the more deprived we feel and the more we feel entitled to a yacht.

In the 1950s, a Harvard sociologist named Samuel Stouffer started theorising the concept he called 'relative deprivation'. He demonstrated that the more an American soldier felt he was entitled to promotion, the more deprived he felt when he didn't get it.

Unlike the yacht scenario, feelings of relative deprivation can be very much justified. Relative deprivation has spurred certain groups to highlight harmful inequalities and start social-justice movements. Women who didn't have the right to vote felt deprived in comparison to men who did. Poorly paid domestic workers felt deprived relative to workers in other industries and agitated for better conditions.

Materialistic relative deprivation, rather than deprivation based on moral rights, seems much more subjective. Obviously, not having access to secure housing is absolute deprivation, but then there are also people who feel deprived because they cannot afford a house with two bathrooms and a separate bedroom for each child. Single-income families can feel deprived compared to dual-income families even though in many instances they can technically afford to live on one income. A dual-income family may be able to afford a bigger house or better holidays – their wealth and professional success is easily observed where the successes of a single-income family are private.

The more dual-income families there are, the bigger the houses and flashier holidays we are frequently exposed to. Eventually, social comparison wins out and we transition to a dual-income to 'keep up'. If we experience relative deprivation for long enough, we actually feel deprived. Even a billionaire can feel relatively deprived in certain company. Shockingly, research shows relative deprivation has more negative health outcomes than actual deprivation. Whether or not you actually are deprived becomes irrelevant if you feel like a pauper.

Increased feelings of relative deprivation have been linked with increased suicide rates, crime, and hostile sexism. Feeling relatively deprived can also reduce impulse control and thus creates vicious cycles in health and financial wellbeing. Less ability to delay gratification often means low-income individuals make constant smaller purchases to ease the discomfort. People who feel deprived are more likely to have difficulty controlling their substance use or dietary choices, which then creates more disadvantage and relative deprivation.

In the developed world, relative deprivation has much more relevance to policy development and societal woes than absolute deprivation. The distress is real in parts of the population that are relatively deprived and this has led to the emergence of middle-class welfare and increased social support. The more wealth is accumulated at the upper end, the more the deprived group will demand to be elevated in society. In 2022, researchers for China's National Health Commission showed that increased social support did successfully mitigate many of the negative impacts of relative deprivation.

Relative deprivation has also spawned the practice of gratitude journaling, which has been shown to improve mental-health outcomes. Social support will only get us so far as relative deprivation is unable to be eliminated in capitalistic society. It could even be considered a prerequisite – the source of the drive to accumulate wealth. People will need tools to reduce their propensity for social comparison and thus reduce their sensitivity to relative deprivation.

Advertising and marketing also actively encourage social comparison and inflame feelings of relative deprivation. Since the insidious and ubiquitous nature of advertising is unlikely to change, we can expect relative deprivation to continue to pose problems in wider society. We can limit our exposure to advertising but we cannot ever truly be free of it.

A few months ago my toddler broke the screen on our ageing, non-smart television. We continued using it for a few weeks with half the screen working but eventually the whole screen went and we had a very large black radio. Apparently, the stores don't sell TVs that aren't internet enabled anymore, so we got our first 'smart' TV. We felt like we had moved into the space age overnight. It was luxurious for the first few weeks, being able to watch whatever we wanted at any given moment. But now it is just our normal TV. We don't know how we lived before. If we went back to a dumb TV we would almost certainly feel deprived.

The majority of people own a smart TV in Australia. Approximately 85% of the global population own a smart phone, at an average cost of approximately $600 per handset. Australia's average house size has doubled since the 1950s and we now have the biggest houses in the world. We spend more on powering and heating and cooling bigger homes. We are one of the largest markets for online fashion retailers, and in 2015 we were ranked the top spending nation in the world by statistics website Statista. When excessive lifestyles become the norm and are overrepresented on social media, the natural human response is to be excessive and feel deprived if you are not.

Increasing social supports is highly effective in addressing *absolute* deprivation but it can only ever be a band-aid for the moving target that is *relative* deprivation. People become accustomed to increased welfare, expect it, and then feel deprived if they don't get it. Prices of goods and services can also respond to welfare increases. A clear example of this in Australia was the National Disability Insurance Scheme (NDIS), which saw providers increase charges for clients with an NDIS plan. Injections of welfare cash such as the NDIS inevitably end up in profit-making systems. When significant social supports are paid directly to a large percentage of the population, it increases their buying power, price competition, and leads to price rises in response.

The most powerful mitigator of relative deprivation is not more money, it's the awareness that you are not actually deprived.

It is absolutely vital that we tease out the wants and the needs in this situation, because financial support cannot realistically extend to people who have a preference to live in a large home and have a bedroom for each of their children. This is not how welfare works. It is irresponsible to spend taxpayer dollars subsidising childcare for families who earn up to half a million dollars annually.

There is also the question of value systems and cultural norms driving our attitudes to spending and our idea of how much is necessary. We live in a culture that values material wealth and professional success, a culture that fails to define work outside of capitalist metrics. Many parents who find the ability to step outside of these value systems that so often don't actually bring happiness or contentment, miraculously find ways to spend more time with their children. If they have the information and the support to realise that time with their children is a serious priority, they make it happen.

In 2023, I interviewed a bunch of families for an article I wrote for

Mamamia[117]. I wanted to know exactly how families were arranging to have a stay-at-home parent in these economic conditions. Contrary to the popular belief that families with a stay-at-home parent are wealthy and old fashioned, we heard from many middle-income families who were cutting their own path to live on a single or dual part-time income. Common features of single-income families appear to be living in rural areas, delaying buying a home, cutting back on spending and negotiating with employers for flexible or unorthodox arrangements.

Here are some of responses:

Living rurally

"My husband and I do 50/50 at home with the kids. Our rent is $420 per week and it works because we are freelancers living in a tiny rural town." *~Rose*

"We negotiated a Sunday-Monday weekend for my partner so he cares for the baby on Mondays and I go to my paid job. Our employer has been very flexible because we work in a remote area, they are so grateful to have competent workers." *~Lucy*

"We relocated out of the city where homes are at least a million dollars to where we bought a house on a much bigger block for $320,000. We no longer need two incomes to survive with four kids." *~Sasha*

"For many rural families, dual incomes are not an option. For me, driving the 50 minutes one day to put my kids into care and then onto work just isn't feasible." *~Jess*

"We moved to work on a remote cattle station so the kids could be with me while I work part-time cooking and gardening." *~Anna*

Work flexibility

"I work 16 hours a week in a well-paid job that has flexibility, paid parental leave and was worth holding onto. My partner runs his own business and also has flexibility." ~*Grace*

"My husband would get home from work at 4pm and we would swap. I would work a 5pm to midnight shift. It was tough but worth having one of us with the kids at all times." ~*Rosie*

"I work 30 hours per fortnight, 6:30am to 9:30am Monday to Friday. I asked for flexibility with work hours and my partner starts a half hour later at 10am." ~*Lisa*

Cutting back spending

"Any extra or unexpected cost takes a long time to recover from financially, we're lucky to save $25-$50 a week. If the rent went up, we'd have to leave our jobs and move interstate to live with our parents." ~*Lucy*

"Camping holidays only, we hardly ever eat out." ~*Sasha*

"Lots of my friends have kept their eldest in childcare when the new baby is born but we have kept our eldest home." ~*Bonnie*

"We have the same second-hand car we bought 13 years ago." ~*Olivia*

"We live much more frugally than other friends my age. We go on very local trips and rarely go out to eat. We have to make our own fun and often that's super cheap." ~*Rose*

Delayed home buying

"Buying a home is on the back burner for us." ~*Lucy*

"We've put off buying our own home because there's no way we can afford to. Not a lot of security but it's what we decided." ~*Jasmine*

"We delayed our home purchase and rented for six years." ~*Shelley*

While many felt there was an element of struggle, they overwhelmingly believed the benefits of having more time with family outweighed the drawbacks. The families we spoke to didn't experience deprivation of basic needs like food, water, clothing and shelter, but several felt a level of deprivation relative to what their family and friends could afford. For example, not being able to afford to eat at a restaurant feels worse if all your friends go out for dinner.

When feelings of relative deprivation emerge on a broad scale they can lead to political unrest or social movements to demand better welfare or rights. Opting to earn more money can reassure us that our kids aren't 'missing out' in a material sense or that we are not being left behind financially compared to our peers. The families I spoke to overcame the sense of relative deprivation by remaining clear about their values and their goals of having more family time.

"The pull to earn more money is strong and we have to remind ourselves of why we made these choices and what's important to our family." ~*Christene*

"We are cash poor but rich in family activities, we have less discretionary spending but hang out with our kids every day." ~*Denielle*.

"It's been really hard but I'm so glad we chose this path." ~*Shelley*

In a sense, these families are de-growthers on a micro scale or individual level. They set limits on how much money they spent and how much they could work while maintaining their own physical or mental health. Their arrangements often relied upon more gender-equitable unpaid care contributions, though some arrangements also accommodated a desire to breastfeed or take on more of unpaid care work if it was a preference for one parent.

There is also the growing trend of non-standard work hours and working from home or even bringing kids to work. Growing waitlists for daycare and preschool mean parents are increasingly arranging to bring their kids to work. In childcare deserts or when family support networks are unavailable, parents can find themselves with few options. Some families are also opting out of daycare due to affordability issues and quality concerns related to the national shortage of educators.

Kayla (last name withheld) is an Executive Assistant for the ACT government who combines working from home with bringing her son to the workplace. "They have an entire kitchen, playroom, TV and feeding room, which is amazing," she explains. "I found daycare way too expensive for my budget and I wanted to be with my son day to day, so I feel very blessed."

Kayla attributes the success of her arrangement to the supportive culture of upper management and also the layout of her building. "The building itself is very family friendly and I'm lucky enough to have a boss who supports me still being the sole carer of my son. I do feel like I'm treading water but I'm sure most parents feel like that at times so I just try to do as much as I can."

While some workplaces pose safety risks to children, many parents like Kayla are finding the arrangement to be safe and with benefits that outweigh the drawbacks.

It's not just parents in office jobs working with kids in tow. Mamamia heard from midwives, vets, farmers, teachers and filmmakers who had arrangements where their kids were present at their workplace. Many parents in regional areas lacked access to formal childcare arrangements, which resulted in their children being present at their place of work.

"I work with my children daily because we're self-employed on the land," Ellen explains. "It's not easy, we're constantly making modifications to keep our children safe, and realistically we have no choice but to accept that this hampers productivity."

Some parents experience support and workplaces that are inclusive of children while others find children are not welcome. In 2023, a pilot program was introduced in the US state of Arkansas, which allowed government departmental employees to bring their children to work under certain circumstances. The trend is signalling a promising shift away from traditional Western cultural beliefs that the care of children is strictly a private responsibility. The idea that caring for young children is a collective, social responsibility—evident in the frequently quoted phrase 'It takes a village to raise a child'—could be key to developing alternative and flexible care arrangements.

Child development experts have pointed out that there are clear benefits of having children more included in their parents' daily work life. Research from the University of Minnesota found that contributing to family life at preschool age was the best predictor for success in adulthood. Children often thrive on exposure to work communities and having a degree of responsibility. Ellen believes her children have benefited from being included in her workplace. "I have a four year old who is more capable than most nine year olds, is responsible, and understands the natural world and where food comes from better than many adults," she explains.

Children being totally absent from workplaces is a relatively recent development of modern society, with children historically being included in aspects of a family's work life. Obviously, there are instances where child labour is harmful and illegal, but zero tolerance for children in the workplace can rob them of a valuable learning tool and a chance to see work role-modelled in real time. It may also help with separation and their concept of where parents go when they are 'at work'.

Anthropologist Sarah Blaffer Hrdy studies communal child-rearing practices which allow adults to work while remaining in the proximity of their children. She told the *New York Times* that the future of the planet depended on improving care models for children. "The conflict is not between maternal feelings and ambitiousness, but between the needs of a human infant for constant, attentive, extended care; and the fact that a woman's ambitions must be played out in workplaces with no tolerance for children."

With a formal childcare system under pressure and shrinking 'village' or family support systems, a future where kids are more commonly included in workplaces may be more realistic than we first think. If work is our life—out of necessity or by choice—then children will need to be included to some extent. As our lives become increasingly work centric and our social networks develop in the workplace, the line between work and family is increasingly blurred. It seems natural that family life might bleed into the workplace in the same way that we bring work home.

It is an extremely complex macro- and micro-economic situation but there remains an obvious need to reconsider how appropriate a dual-income society really is, how the economy will continue to function as we reach the limits of human capital, and a need to investigate ways to mitigate conditions that leave families unwell and disconnected. Still, many childcare advocates and families who believe there is no alternative continue to use the financial argument to close down the debate – we have no choice therefore we must use systems like childcare and, if there are negative consequences of this, those consequences are unavoidable and should not be discussed.

In an interview on ABC radio, childcare advocate Georgie Dent, put this argument forward plainly. She represented a dominant viewpoint expressed among government and childcare advocates which seems to be that we should not acknowledge the evidence-based risks of childcare because it will make parents feel bad. "We know that for a lot of families you cannot provide for your family if you can't access paid work and we, sort of, punish families for being in that position when we say, when we create the narrative that says you're somehow doing the wrong thing if you're not able to make sacrifices so that one of you can stay."

Firstly, it's the experience of separation that informs the narrative that something is wrong when we spend large parts of the day without our children. Secondly, the evidence informing this narrative is a neutral source of information. It's not that researchers want to 'punish families'.

Dent went even further, saying that providing support for families so they weren't forced to enrol their children in childcare was 'unrealistic'. "We know that single-parent households do not have that luxury, we know we don't have the broad safety net that would make it easier for a lot of families to sort of choose not to work and so we've got to be realistic and early education is one of the… it is the most transformative social and economic reform we can pursue."

No, we don't have a broad safety net. But we most certainly should.

Is it a luxury for a baby to have access to its parents throughout the day? It seems like a basic human right being cast as a luxury in order to justify not supporting parents in the work of caring for their kids. Is it not a realistic expectation that single parents might receive adequate support to care for their own children? Is it ethical to simply tell them to 'get a real job'? A broad safety net that would make it easier for families to choose to look after their children seems exactly what we need. Why does Dent dismiss it as so out of reach?

Not only does this ignore whole swathes of evidence about how stressed parents are financially (even on dual incomes), how financial stress affects kids, how the brain develops and how our environments in the early years can contribute to mental illness later in life, but it actively dismisses the role of parental caregivers as quite unnecessary in the day-to-day life of children. Dent is well-intentioned but her blinkered advocacy for childcare prevents her from seeing the full picture.

The bottom line is that it is inhumane and unethical to accept this lack of choice and freedom in who cares for our children. Our only realistic option should be policy that supports the ability to care for ourselves and our children, to preserve the ability to maintain our own health and wellbeing. Dent wrote about the importance of maintaining personal wellbeing in her book *Breaking Badly* in which she charts her own nervous breakdown at the age of 25. She actually delayed writing the book while pregnant with her third child due to concerns about the impact on her own wellbeing that an increased workload would have with two older children and a young baby. 'As much as I wanted to author a book at some point, the only project I really wanted to be consumed by at that time was my baby and our growing family,' she wrote in *Women's Agenda*. 'I pressed pause on the project, in part probably, due to the regard I had for my own wellbeing and mental health, regard I only developed because I fell apart badly after neglecting both for too long.'

On the one hand, Dent is all too aware that the mental-health consequences of overwork can be dire, but on the other hand, she fails to recognise how dual-income lifestyles are feeding the problem of overwork. She argues the dual-income society is inevitable. We owe it to families to be transparent, to be innovative with policy, and to look outside the childcare square when it comes to relieving financial pressure.

What is sold to parents as financial empowerment is actually a well-documented trap. Dismissing this trap—and the lack of choice that comes with it—as unavoidable removes all accountability on behalf of government, workplaces, and individuals themselves to seek alternatives. Steady-state economies with birth rates stabilised at replacement rate must be a clear priority for governments. This can only be achieved with careful, intentional planning for a future where we don't remain slaves to an ever-growing economy. Any future periods of strong growth and the more affordable living standards they promise can only be short lived as prices inevitably adjust and inflate to capitalise on higher incomes. Welfare and social or family support payments are important short-term solutions, but unless it is coupled with long-term planning to stabilise economies and populations, it is nothing but a band-aid effect that exacerbates problems arising under constant growth systems.

CHAPTER FIFTEEN

The End of Elitist Feminism

When American suffragettes raised their banners on a wintry day in Washington in 1913 they were ill-prepared on two fronts. First, they underestimated the number of spectators who would show up on Pennsylvania Avenue to watch them march toward the great white dome of the Capitol Building. Thousands came to see the staged spectacle, many of whom were hostile to their cause and succeeded in blocking their passageway until the army showed up to clear a path.

Their second underestimation was the determination of Black women to participate. The organisers of that famous rally had made a concerted effort to exclude Black women from the march through deterring them from registering. Black women just didn't fit the image they were trying to portray with the carefully orchestrated rally, a sea of white, purple and gold famously led by lawyer Inez Milholland Boissevain dressed in a flowing white cape astride a magnificent white horse. It was a vision of purity in a brave new world and they didn't want racial or other human rights issues detracting from that.

Koa Beck explores this day in her book, *White Feminism*. She writes that on the morning of the march, organisers from the National American Women's Suffrage Association insisted that coloured women march at the back of the procession and separately to white women in order to preserve the organisation's support from wealthy donors in the Deep South. Alice Paul, Chair of NAWSA, wrote of the segregation, 'I cannot see ... that having this procession without their participation is in any way injuring them in the least.'

The inclusion of the 19th Amendment to the US constitution granting women suffrage was a hollow victory for Black women, who would be deterred from voting polls due to racial violence for many years to come. It was certainly not a victory for Black women who were unable to vote due to illiteracy. Similar scenes played out in Australia where Aboriginal and Torres Strait Islander Peoples would not have the right to vote until the 1960s. Gender-equality movements in Western nations have been characterised by a strategy of ignoring glaring social inequities in order to achieve immediate gains for a select few. This is why I cannot accept the current terms of equality that are on the table; I will not leave women behind and I will not pretend to be something I am not.

The metaphorical procession of white feminists has continued throughout the decades and into the 21st century. Women of colour would again seek the support of white feminists during the second wave of feminism in the 1960s in a desperate attempt to seek better conditions for the domestic and care workers who were enabling wealthy white women to work outside the home. White feminists would, once again, see the Black feminist's agenda as a threat to the success of their own cause and exclude their women-of-colour counterparts from the movement. If labour wasn't cheap, it was harder to justify women working outside the home. White feminists refused to be party to advocacy that would make the hired help more expensive.

Exclusionary tactics have become a permanent feature of the women's movement and continue to hamper progress for marginalised and disadvantaged women. Just as members of NAWSA failed to see that true progress needed to include all women, girlboss feminists continue to act in their own self-interest and fail to advocate for measures that benefit all women. George Orwell would later satirise this dangerous phenomenon of two-speed liberation movements in his classic *Animal Farm* with the line, 'All animals are equal, but some are more equal than others.'

Like the Bolsheviks who overthrew the Russian aristocracy and then proceeded to emulate them in many ways, white feminists became part of a new ruling class but instead of using their new position to tear down the structures that had excluded them and devalued them for so long, they preserved them for their own benefit. They emulated the men who made up those power structures, right down to the starch in their suit jackets, the tenor of their voices, the childlessness… or at least the appearance of childlessness.

The exclusion feminists perpetuated was not simply a measure of expediency but a necessary precondition of the movement. This is because the liberation of elite women was entirely contingent on the existence of a lower class of people who would continue to do the work they could afford not to do. As Koa Beck explains in *White Feminism*, it is a system of perennially shifting care work onto someone else. It's a system of eat or be eaten.

Even today, caregivers remain largely excluded because they continue to threaten the agenda of mainstream feminism in the same way Black women did in the 1960s. Supporting unpaid caregivers does not enable white feminists to achieve their goal of increasing female workforce participation, while supporting paid care work threatens affordability of the childcare they rely on to work outside the home.

The strategy of steadily replacing unpaid care work with commodified care lessens the disadvantage somewhat, because at least the carer is being paid a meagre wage, but at its core paid care work remains an instrument to facilitate people doing work that is better valued and better paid if they are at all able to do so. Feminism simply created the conditions whereby women could avoid disadvantageous work but it did breathtakingly little to remedy the true cause of female oppression – the devaluation of women's work.

In many cases, the feminist movement overtly denigrated acts of care to justify their cause and in doing so, did care work and those who engaged in it a grave disservice. Betty Friedan went as far as to call women in caregiving roles less evolved. Popular culture dehumanised caregivers in *Stepford Wives*. Rights for women have time and again been won at the expense of caregivers, by excluding them, trivialising care work as non-essential while characterising the people who perform it as sad and unintelligent. While calling women to elevate their status and grasp equality, feminists simultaneously perpetuated value systems and beliefs that deprioritised certain women thus ensuring a lower class to take on the work that was now beneath them.

The problem is that what has been characterised as lowly work—the raising of babies and children during the most developmentally vulnerable stage of their life—is actually critical work. Most feminists today realise the misstep but struggle to reconcile their disdain for care work with truly valuing the people who do it. This contradiction is not unique to women's movements, with South African politician Christiaan de Wet identifying the same conflict in Roman societies, writing, 'It is ironic that despite the view that they were incompetent and degenerate, slaves played a major role in the rearing and education of the elite children of the Roman household.'

Fast forward to October 23rd 2023, and two prominent, elite white women faced a pack of reporters in Australia to deliver a long-awaited plan to fast-track gender equality on a national level. The report was put together over several years by the Women's Economic Equality Taskforce and hailed as a kind of enzyme that could speed up the catalysts of change. It was a red-letter day for feminism. About 60 seconds into her address, the Minister for Women, Katy Gallagher, revealed her inner white feminist with three simple words: "women work less".

What Gallagher meant was 'women do less of the work that is paid' but the content of the report made it clear that she and the taskforce members also believed that women in caregiving roles are worth less to society. If Gallagher believed that unpaid care work was a valuable and necessary contribution, the report would have been full of recommendations on how to better support the contribution that is unpaid care work. Instead, Gallagher supported the recommendations that mean to remedy the perceived 'women working less' by minimising their unpaid contributions. If unpaid care work is easily discarded, it is not of value.

The taskforce promised billions of dollars to the economy if government could create the conditions that meant all women could largely avoid unpaid care work. They recommended getting women into paid work both as an antidote to their own financial and social disadvantage but also to the problem of lagging productivity. The words Gallagher used are important because, even if the intended meaning is more complex, when we hear the phrase 'women work less' over and over out of the mouths of people in positions of authority, we come to believe it in a literal sense. We internalise that, we start to believe that care work isn't real work and, ultimately, we devalue ourselves.

As the white suffragettes had disenfranchised Black women, in a flourish, Gallagher excluded the hundreds of thousands of Australian women who perform unpaid work every day. Chair of the taskforce, Sam Mostyn, would echo these sentiments later in the press conference by saying, "I just don't know who is prepared today to continue to bear the cost of … women not using their education, or us not utilising half of the population at the time that we need productivity lifted, it's an available asset, very simple levers to be pulled."

Women in caregiving roles are reduced to assets and dollar signs, they are characterised as a burden and wasted resource, and their contributions to society are only counted if they play out in the workplace. In cold, economic terms Mostyn told Australian women that care work was a waste of their life. It's easier for white feminists to externalise the problem and make it into an exercise of 'fixing other women' rather than interrogating their own internalised misogyny and the way that is playing out for them.

Lawyer and celebrated author Bri Lee identifies this age-old tendency to blame people for their disadvantage rather than interrogate the economic and social constructs that create disadvantage in her book *Who Gets to be Smart*. 'Rich people continue to believe the poor simply don't work hard enough ... all the while, the people at the top dictate what legitimate knowledge looks and sounds like.'

Gallagher and women in power are telling other women if they just work a bit harder or smarter, if they simply 'go back to work', they can be equal. If they just do the right kind of work, they can garner respect.

There is a line in the Australian musical drama, *The Sapphires*, where a dual-heritage sister sent to a private school in the city returns to visit her home with a newly acquired disdain for her relatives. On the river-bank, Kay says, "If you people worked as much as you fished, you'd be really rich, you know?" Kay represents the 'enlightened feminist' telling the masses what is good for them. It's the same blindness to the systemic and contextual factors that disadvantage the oppressed class, instead blaming poor 'choices', work ethic or lack of ambition for their disadvantage.

What if the compulsion for a woman to care for a baby she just birthed is as strong as the connection to country or the desire to live in community? Will forcing mothers of young children into full-time work later be seen as a gross incursion on individual liberties and the basic human right to give and receive care?

The disconnect between women in power and grassroots women is as shocking today as it was in 1913. Feminism is failing to shift the dial on cultural belief systems that devalue care work and those who do it because feminists who are calling the shots have internalised a devaluation of care. They perpetuate it. Many women, publicly and privately, don't actually want to drink the productivity Kool-Aid the feminist elite are handing out. Childcare is being presented as the only option available, but true freedom for all women can only be achieved when both free childcare and/or financial support while raising young children are on offer.

Perhaps the deepest contradiction of modern white feminism is the outward show of support for women less powerful and less affluent than themselves, but the failure to practically implement systems that would actually benefit those women. White feminists have become much more adept at hiding their whiteness or conservatism. Rather than public segregation, it's now a show of altruism where they invite other women to play career musical chairs knowing full well there aren't enough chairs to go around or that not all women can or want to play.

Evidence of the conservative core plays out in other ways; for example, where typically left-leaning feminists might usually acknowledge that ecological resources are finite they advocate for policies aimed at endless economic growth. Where modern-day feminists have lent support to left-leaning movements that seek to preserve the intrinsic value of things like environment, arts and culture, love and care, and human rights, they also seem conveniently blind to the commodification of childhood and fail to consider children's rights. Karl Marx extensively critiqued the commodification of society as a phenomenon that obscures the true value of contributions by reducing them to market value.

Feminists try to ameliorate the conservatism of commodifying every last inch of life on Earth with politically correct lines about better valuing early educators, women's empowerment and improving quality of care, which is at least in part motivated by a desire to protect their own children from the ill effects of poor quality institutional group-care situations. White feminism dictates that care is only worthwhile if it's paid, while left-leaning ideologies applied in other care situations such as disability, mental illness, and aged care recognise the intangible value of being cared for by family at home. With respect to children and babies, white feminists are able to ignore the way commodification erodes the essence of care and the benefits it can confer to the people who receive it.

The modern-day equivalent to white feminists deciding their right to vote was more important than women of colour feeling safe in the streets is that elite feminists have now decided that their right to childcare is more important than a woman's right to care for her own children. Women who want to perform care work and be supported in that are a threat to the elite feminists' agenda of equalising workforce participation at all costs. As Kim Hong Nguyen puts it in her new book *Mean Girl Feminism*, these 'white ladies of liberal reason' are failing spectacularly to understand the pluralistic attitudes to family life. They 'whitesplain' the economic benefits of all women outsourcing the care of their younger children, apparently oblivious to cultural and social reasons outside of economics that might influence a woman's decision.

Feminists, and specifically women in power in Australia, were complicit in the erosion of supports for single mothers. At the time, former Prime Minister Julia Gillard said that in cutting payments for single mothers she was actually gifting them the dignity of 'work'. It is clear from her reasoning that she felt caregiving was therefore undignified. Where the single parent is constantly and rightly framed by the feminist Left as someone in a position of disadvantage and requiring support, the white lady of liberal reason views caregiving as unemployment.

Even women in power will be forever frustrated with the structural and cultural barriers that remain, simply because they are not men. They will lament the way people still judge them by their appearance or characterise them as less competent leaders, but they accepted these terms when they assimilated into a system that did not intrinsically value women and their unique contributions or perspectives, but instead demanded they morph into a new version of themselves. Women in power have been complicit in these characterisations of women, have weaponised them and consistently apply them to women in unpaid caregiving roles. And now white feminism isn't even working well for its architects.

Feminism is running out of fuel because it's not enough to simply be a woman and assume a position of power and influence, we need men and women in leadership who understand care as a valuable contribution worthy of support. We need leaders who have wanted to prioritise the care of their young children but have been robbed of that basic right. We need leaders who were able to prioritise the care of young children and come out the other side with the conviction to create the support they didn't have.

The clear message Ireland recently sent to the feminist elite the world over is that the masses will not tolerate the erasure of womanhood or mothers[118]. Women want to be acknowledged and supported in their role of caring for babies and young children. The steady march of feminists arm-in-arm with so-called progressives can no longer get away with leaving everyday women behind.

A referendum[119] to erase a woman's work in the home from the Irish constitution was rejected by 74% of voters. The overwhelming No vote is a frightening insight into just how out of touch people in positions of leadership can be with the general population. It cost

Ireland €23m ($38.1m) to indulge the ideological aspirations of a small minority who wish to erase mothers and erode a woman's right to care for her children.

The referendum proposed to remove part of Article 41, which reads: 'The State recognises that by her life within the home, woman gives to the State a support without which the common good cannot be achieved. The State shall, therefore, endeavour to ensure that mothers shall not be obliged by economic necessity to engage in labour to the neglect of their duties in the home.'

This section was to be replaced with gender-neutral phrasing that erased 'woman' and 'mother' but also appeared to reduce the state's obligation to support women in the foundational work of care. The amended section read: 'The State recognises that the provision of care, by members of a family to one another by reason of the bonds that exist among them, gives to Society a support without which the common good cannot be achieved, and shall strive to support such provision.'

It's not just a matter of constitutional semantics that the Irish public voted on – they voted on how women should be valued in society, their visibility, and how their unpaid work should be supported. The public wish to retain the constitution in its current form because it protects a woman's right to work both outside and inside the home, as long as the decision is made freely. Under the current economic and policy conditions, it's the woman's right to work inside the home that is most at risk.

The people of Ireland wish to safeguard and support a mother's right to care for her family. Whether or not the Irish government, or any nation, is capable of upholding such an obligation is another question entirely. The message from mothers across the world has been loud and clear for decades – we can't afford not to return to paid work. In the face of this gross incursion upon a woman's freedom of choice, most nations simply promoted this as the new norm and 'economic growth'. A woman's work in the home was framed as an unnecessary luxury. Not in Ireland.

Ireland's care referendum could be considered valuable as a rare case study that demonstrates the disconnect between elite career women who influence policy and the masses of women with jobs who have to live out the reality of the policy. It's astonishing what happens when the views of everyday people are actually publicly aired and taken into consideration. The chasm between what the top end of town thought was good for women and what grassroots women actually want was wider than anyone could have predicted.

The results in Ireland alone hint at a kind of democratisation of the women's rights movement now playing out across the internet. Mothers working inside the home now carry a tiny handheld portal to government hearings, parenting forums, social media platforms, national discussions, and political debate.

Women engaging in care work inside the home are no longer locked out of public debate and cultural influence. Platforms and discussions that were once the sole domain of professionals and leaders are slowly being colonised by grassroots people. The smartphone, and the occasional referendum, are making their views impossible to ignore or overlook. We have good evidence to suggest the era of elitist feminists reigning supreme is coming to an end.

CHAPTER SIXTEEN

Conclusion

I don't have all the answers. While many of the solutions offered in this book are real and actionable, many are thought-experiments that need to be challenged and refined or put back on the shelf. It is through this process of engaging with new ideas and putting our heads together that we will produce the best solutions and achieve true progress. If there is one point I've made here that gives you an idea and you pursue it, that's a win for me. I hope that you never stop trying to approach a problem from a new angle. Turn it over in your hands again and again until you see something you didn't see before.

The other key message is take care to correctly define the problem. Make sure you are asking the right questions. There is often pushback against wallowing in the problems because it's painful and people are so hungry for answers or a quick fix but we have to know and understand the complexities of the problem intimately in order to find appropriate solutions.

I tried not to be mean-spirited but sometimes the hurt and frustration spills out. I hope you can appreciate that accountability is absolutely critical in moving forward. Mistakes have been made, and a lot of people have been left behind. If we don't call it out, it will keep happening.

Choice is the only true liberator and as long as we don't have that we must go back to the drawing board again and again. Increases to paid parental leave and parenting payments can better facilitate choice, but policy change alone is not enough. Genuine liberation—genuine *choice*—comes from a process of culturally legitimising the choice to care. It is a process of undoing the damage to the image of care that feminist, capitalist, and neoliberal forces have inflicted over many decades. It is only when the choice to care is culturally sanctioned and defended by those around us, that parents will feel true freedom to engage in this vital labour. It's not a choice to be made freely while public discourses and private conversations present parents who engage in care work as lazy, selfish, less educated, indulgent, not contributing or depriving their babies and toddlers of optimal education and social development.

Increases in payments to support parenting must also be accompanied by a reassessment of our own values. We must reassess the point at which having no genuine choice bleeds into a preference for a higher standard of living beyond what is perhaps necessary for our wellbeing and the development of our children. We have to be transparent about what is real lack of choice and honest about whether we are using 'lack of choice' to mask preferences to engage in paid work and accumulate wealth or material goods.

If true wealth is obtained from security and safety in our earliest relationships, a foundation from which we can then function and succeed in society, maybe we can be satisfied that creating a better future for our children isn't only achieved through financial gain. There are obvious instances in which people who find themselves in very fortunate circumstances in a material sense are often plagued by deep-seated emotional insecurities. Many a billionaire has spoken of the desire to trade wealth for things that money can't buy – time, healthy interpersonal relationships, immortality. It's been said before, money isn't everything.

Support payments must be carefully planned in an environment of hyper-consumerism fuelled by social media comparisons alongside insidious and ever-present marketing forces. In an environment where we are increasingly incapable of distinguishing between our wants and needs. The emergence of a dual-income class has inflated prices no doubt, but it has also inflated our expectations of what we are entitled to. The cultural changes that are necessary rely on language changes and the development of the ability to exercise critical thought or discretion when it comes to social pressures that result in overspending.

The second major point of this book is to demonstrate that care systems must undergo a process of overhaul that limits the capacity for profits to determine the care our children receive. We can only do this, we can only generate the will to change if we are completely clear on the consequences of letting profits govern the care our vulnerable receive.

It is a matter of absolute urgency that outcomes for mothers and children are improved. We must accept that childhood outcomes and maternal health are worsening, and have grown worse, in a context of increasing prevalence of childcare and dual-income lifestyles – the very elements that were meant to improve the wellbeing of women and children.

As a general rule, the gender equality movement has confused equal treatment with equitable treatment. Women deserve every opportunity, but we cannot continue to be treated like men and play by rules that were designed for men.

I have often wondered why I have gone to such great lengths, at my own expense and at the expense of my children, to examine these issues and highlight the flawed nature of our approach. Why did I choose this hill to die on? Am I insecure about my own choices and desperate to prove I've made the right ones? Quite the opposite. I think this book was motivated through the honesty of knowing how imperfect I am as a parent and being able to identify that there were factors that no doubt contributed to my inability to deliver adequate care at times. I am motivated by the overwhelming desire to change those conditions for my own children and for future generations more broadly.

Ultimately, one of the strongest motivators was my inability to withstand misinformation. I am working on my ability to entertain the perspectives of others, understand how I can learn from people from different backgrounds, but I will not, under any circumstances, accept the proliferation of information that is simply wrong. Especially not when that information is motivated by profit. The assertion that we can achieve gender equality by outsourcing care and also adequately meet the needs of mothers and children is wrong. I proved that with available evidence. Every time this false claim is peddled out, I hope it can be called out for the lie it is.

Finally, one of my personal quirks is an ever-present awareness of my own mortality. Most of us have a fairly good ability to ignore this fact of life completely, bar the attendance at a funeral or the anniversary of a loved one's passing. My dad died in a car accident before I was born and one of my formative understandings of life is that not everyone gets to watch their children grow up. You can be here one minute, gone the next. Death does not discriminate or wait for the right time. So, I have always been deeply concerned with how my time here is spent. There could be no more important use of our time than the passing on of our love, experience, and knowledge. Anything that threatens our ability to do this should be intensely and regularly scrutinised.

Endnotes

CHAPTER ONE

1 *Understanding the empathy deficit.* (2025). Theaustralian.com.au. https://www.theaustralian.com.au

2 Scatliffe, N., Casavant, S., Vittner, D., & Cong, X. (2019). Oxytocin and Early parent-infant interactions: a Systematic Review. *International Journal of Nursing Sciences*, 6(4), 445-453. https://www.ncbi.nlm.nih.gov/pmc/articles/PMC6838998/

3 Shonkoff, J. P., & Garner, A. S. (2011). The Lifelong Effects of Early Childhood Adversity and Toxic Stress This Article. *American Academy of Pediatrics.* https://doi.org/10.1542/peds.2011-2663)

4 Graham, A. M., Pfeifer, J. H., Fisher, P. A., Lin, W., Gao, W., & Fair, D. A. (2015). The potential of infant fMRI research and the study of early life stress as a promising exemplar. *Developmental Cognitive Neuroscience*, 12, 12-39. https://doi.org/10.1016/j.dcn.2014.09.005

5 Rakers, F., Rupprecht, S., Dreiling, M., Bergmeier, C., Witte, O. W., & Schwab, M. (2017). Transfer of maternal psychosocial stress to the fetus. *Neuroscience & Biobehavioral Reviews, 117.* https://doi.org/10.1016/j.neubiorev.2017.02.019

6 Tapscott, V. (2023, July 25). *"A male commentator was criticised for his comment during the Matildas game. I agree with him."* Mamamia. https://www.mamamia.com.au/matildas-game-male-commentator-katrina-gorry/

CHAPTER TWO

7 Engels, F. (1884). The Origin of the family, Private Property and the State. Sumptibus Publications.

8 Cook, P. (2011). *Mothering matters : the sources of love, and how our culture harms infants, women and society.* (p. 72) Freedom Publishing.

9 Diamond, J. M. (2010). *The worst mistake in the history of the human race* (p. 66). Oplopanax Publishing.

10 Strathearn, L. (2011). Maternal Neglect: Oxytocin, Dopamine and the Neurobiology of Attachment. *Journal of Neuroendocrinology, 23*(11), 1054–1065. https://doi.org/10.1111/j.1365-2826.2011.02228.x

11 Komisar, E. (2017). *Being There*. Penguin.

CHAPTER THREE

12 Sarah Blaffer Hrdy. (2009). *Mothers and Others : the Evolutionary Origins of Mutual Understanding*. Belknap Press Of Harvard University Press.

13 Sutou, S. (2012). Hairless mutation: a driving force of humanization from a human-ape common ancestor by enforcing upright walking while holding a baby with both hands. *Genes to Cells, 17*(4), 264–272. https://doi.org/10.1111/j.1365-2443.2012.01592.x

14 Kohler, J. (2021, December 14). *Julie Kohler.* Julie Kohler. https://www.juliekkohler.com/white-picket-fence-podcast-posts/when-career-feminism-won

15 Waring, M. (2025). *Counting for nothing: What men value and what women are worth: Marilyn Waring*. Marilynwaring.com. https://marilynwaring.com/publications/counting-for-nothing.asp

16 Koa Beck. (2021). *White Feminism*. Simon & Schuster Ltd.

17 Bai, X., Song, Z., Zhou, Y., Wang, X., Wang, Y., & Zhang, D. (2021). Bibliometrics and Visual Analysis of the Research Status and Trends of Postpartum Depression From 2000 to 2020. *Frontiers in Psychology, 12*. https://doi.org/10.3389/fpsyg.2021.665181

CHAPTER FOUR

18 *Mathilde Magazine.* (2023). Issue 5. https://www.mathildemagazine.com/product-page/single-issue-issue-5

19 Tapscott, V. (2023, July 27). *Dominant feminist theory neglects motherhood.* Theaustralian.com.au. https://www.theaustralian.com.au/inquirer/why-does-mainstream-feminism-still-devalue-motherhood/news-story/e63f6b9767f511613ca61fe33a536916

20 *Inquiry Report - A path to universal early childhood education and care.* (2024). Pc.gov.au. https://www.pc.gov.au/inquiries/completed/childhood/report

21 *Budget 2023–24.* (n.d.). Archive.budget.gov.au. https://archive.budget.gov.au/2023-24/index.htm

CHAPTER FIVE

22 Australian Government. (2023). *A 10-year-plan to unleash the full capacity and contribution of women to the Australian economy 2023 - 2033.* Pmc.gov.au. https://www.pmc.gov.au/resources/10-year-plan

23 Tapscott, V. (2025). *Stay-at-home mums are not a drain on the economy.* Theaustralian.com.au. https://www.theaustralian.com.au/inquirer/stayathome-mums-are-not-a-drain-on-the-economy/news-story/129aab78118d3dc703fc163689135f5b

24 Tapscott, V. (2022). *I am being shamed for choosing to stay at home with my kids.* Theaustralian.com.au. https://www.theaustralian.com.au/the-oz/perspective/childcare-is-coercion-dressed-up-as-opportunities-for-women/news-story/4a6d67fdfb01a8d58795807cc246d747

25 Tapscott, V. (2023). *It's time to face facts, childcare isn't improving our quality of life.* Theaustralian.com.au. https://www.theaustralian.com.au/inquirer/its-time-we-back-parents-not-just-childcare/news-story/ace8dda716c16020fa85138b35d1a3e0

26 *How pregnancy rewires the female brain.* Theaustralian.com.au. https://www.theaustralian.com.au/inquirer/science-shatters-the-baby-brain-myth-for-new-mothers/news-story/60733cc99a7e60243f6b37e55cf8dfd2

27 Pawluski, J. (2023). *Mommy Brain.* Demeter Press.

28 Tapscott, V. (2024) *The most concerning element of tradwife bashing.* Theaustralian.com.au. www.theaustralian.com.au

CHAPTER SIX

29 Taylor, T. (2014). Treatment of nausea and vomiting in pregnancy. *VOLUME, 37*(2). https://www.nps.org.au/assets/c54914225deb37a1-077be09b52f0-8b91fd8dbb1142caa58132e34b40b5466d337bd7268dda75dfae4a61d9f6.pdf

30 Thurber, C., Dugas, L. R., Ocobock, C., Carlson, B., Speakman, J. R., & Pontzer, H. (2019). Extreme events reveal an alimentary limit on sustained maximal human energy expenditure. *Science Advances*, 5(6), eaaw0341. https://doi.org/10.1126/sciadv.aaw0341

31 Keedle, H., R.N. Craig Lockwood, Keedle, W., Susic, D., & Dahlen, H. G. (2023). What women want if they were to have another baby: the Australian Birth Experience Study (BESt) cross-sectional national survey. *BMJ Open, 13*(9), e071582–e071582. https://doi.org/10.1136/bmjopen-2023-071582

32 Pelvic Organ Prolapse: One Woman's Journey to Improved Quality of Life - UF Health. (2022). Ufhealth.org. https://ufhealth.org/stories/2022/pelvic-organ-prolapse-one-womans-journey-to-improved-quality-of-life

33 *SELECT COMMITTEE ON BIRTH TRAUMA*. (2024). https://www.parliament.nsw.gov.au/lcdocs/inquiries/2965/FINAL%20Birth%20Trauma%20Report%20-%2029%20April%202024.pdf

34 Allison, J. (2016). *The Golden Month*, Beatnik Publishing

35 *Pelvic Organ Prolapse*. (n.d.). Continence Foundation of Australia. https://www.continence.org.au/who-it-affects/women/prolapse

36 Pearson, C. (2017, January 17). *What The French Get So Right About Taking Care Of New Moms.* HuffPost. https://www.huffpost.com/entry/what-the-french-get-so-right-about-taking-care-of-new-moms_n_587d27b4e4b086022ca939c4

37 Soet, J. E., Brack, G. A., & Dilorio, C. (2003). Prevalence and Predictors of Women's Experience of Psychological Trauma During Childbirth. *Birth, 30*(1), 36–46. https://doi.org/10.1046/j.1523-536x.2003.00215.x

38 UNICEF. (2019, August 1). *Why family-friendly policies are critical to increasing breastfeeding rates worldwide.* https://www.unicef.org/press-releases/why-family-friendly-policies-are-critical-increasing-breastfeeding-rates-worldwide

39 Borra, C., Iacovou, M., & Sevilla, A. (2014). New Evidence on Breastfeeding and Postpartum Depression: The Importance of Understanding Women's Intentions. *Maternal and Child Health Journal, 19*(4), 897–907. https://doi.org/10.1007/s10995-014-1591-z

40 Queensland Health. (2020, May 13). *Importance of breastfeeding.* www.health.qld.gov.au. https://www.health.qld.gov.au/clinical-practice/guidelines-procedures/clinical-staff/maternity/nutrition/breastfeeding/importance

41 Unveiling the predatory tactics of the formula milk industry. (2023). *The Lancet, 0*(0). https://doi.org/10.1016/S0140-6736(23)00118-6

42 Tapscott, V. *Breastfeeding better for planet than being vegan.* Theaustralian.com.au. www.theaustralian.com.au

43 Tapscott, V. (2023) *It's time we back parents, not just childcare.* Theaustralian.com.au. www.theaustralian.com.au

44 (2024). Ifpri.org. https://www.ifpri.org/project/alive-and-thrive/

45 Walters, D. D., Phan, L. T. H., & Mathisen, R. (2019). The cost of not breastfeeding: global results from a new tool. *Health Policy and Planning, 34*(6), 407–417. https://doi.org/10.1093/heapol/czz050

46 *Mostyn heads to Yarralumla, carrying her political baggage.* Theaustralian.com.au. https://www.theaustralian.com.au/inquirer/gender-equal-except-for-singleincome-families/news-story/63deeb8e86c634e9c2570db99548d8c0

CHAPTER SEVEN

47 Sarah Blaffer Hrdy. (2009). *Mothers and Others : the Evolutionary Origins of Mutual Understanding.* Belknap Press Of Harvard University Press.

48 Allison, J. (2016). *The Golden Month*, Beatnik Publishing

49 Meadows, D. H., Meadows, D. L., Randers, J., & Behrens III, W. W. (1972). *The Limits to Growth: A report for the Club of Rome's project on the predicament of mankind.* Universe Books.

50 Jensen, J. F., Tønnesen, L. L., Söderström, M., Thorsen, H., & Siersma, V. (2010). Paracetamol for feverish children: parental motives and experiences. *Scandinavian Journal of Primary Health Care, 28*(2), 115–120. https://doi.org/10.3109/02813432.2010.487346

51 Tapscott, V. (2024). *Painful truth about how we over-medicate our children.* Theaustralian.com.au. www.theaustralian.com.au

52 Walters, D. D., Phan, L. T. H., & Mathisen, R. (2019). The cost of not breastfeeding: global results from a new tool. *Health Policy and Planning, 34*(6), 407–417. https://doi.org/10.1093/heapol/czz050

53 Prater, E. (2023, February 7). *Big Formula's "exploitative" marketing tactics prey on new parents' fears, experts say.* Fortune Well. https://fortune.com/well/2023/02/07/big-formulas-exploitative-marketing-tactics-prey-parents-fears/

CHAPTER EIGHT

54 Tapscott, V. (2025). *We're both working but only one of us is paid.* Theaustralian.com.au. www.theaustralian.com.au

55 Tapscott, V. (2023). *Farmers look down the barrel of another big dry.* Theaustralian.com.au. www.theaustralian.com.au

56 Kuttner, R. (1999). *Everything for Sale: The Virtues and Limits of Markets*, University Of Chicago Press

CHAPTER NINE

57 Kvalvaag, A. M. (2023). What Integration Discourses "Do": The Gendered Migratization of Policy Issues and Justification of Welfare Retrenchment. *NORA - Nordic Journal of Feminist and Gender Research, 32*(2), 113–124. https://doi.org/10.1080/08038740.2023.2250345

58 Nikel, D. (2021, April 16). *Parental Leave & Other Benefits in Norway.* Life in Norway. https://www.lifeinnorway.net/parental-leave/

59 Zachrisson, H. D., & Dearing, E. (2014). Family Income Dynamics, Early Childhood Education and Care, and Early Child Behavior Problems in Norway. *Child Development, 86*(2), 425–440. https://doi.org/10.1111/cdev.12306

60 *Inquiry Report - A path to universal early childhood education and care.* (2024). Pc.gov.au. https://www.pc.gov.au/inquiries/completed/childhood/report

CHAPTER TEN

61 Byrne, B., & Little, C. (n.d.). *Preschool and childcare have little impact on a child's later school test scores.* The Conversation. https://theconversation.com/preschool-and-childcare-have-little-impact-on-a-childs-later-school-test-scores-146003

62 *E4Kids.* (2018, November 20). Melbourne Graduate School of Education. https://education.unimelb.edu.au/research/projects/E4Kids

63 Gray-Lobe, G., Pathak, P. A., & Walters, C. R. (2021, May 1). *The Long-Term Effects of Universal Preschool in Boston.* National Bureau of Economic Research. https://www.nber.org/papers/w28756

64 Havnes, T., & Mogstad, M. (2009). No Child Left Behind: Universal Child Care and Children's Long-Run Outcomes. *SSRN Electronic Journal.* https://doi.org/10.2139/ssrn.1506313

65 Chetty, R, et al. (2011). *A. Alfred Taubman Center for State and Local Government.*

66 Deming, D. (2009). Early Childhood Intervention and Life-Cycle Skill Development: Evidence from Head Start. *American Economic Journal: Applied Economics, 1*(3), 111–134. https://www.jstor.org/stable/25760174

67 Cornelissen, T., & Dustmann, C. (2019). Early School Exposure, Test Scores, and Noncognitive Outcomes. *American Economic Journal: Economic Policy, 11*(2), 35–63. https://doi.org/10.1257/pol.20170641

68 Heckman, J. J. (2013). *Giving kids a fair chance.* Cambridge, Mass The Mit Press.

69 Silliman, M., & Virtanen, H. (2022). Labor Market Returns to Vocational Secondary Education. *American Economic Journal: Applied Economics, 14*(1), 197–224. https://doi.org/10.1257/app.20190782

70 Gruber, J., Kosonen, T., & Huttunen, K. (2023). Paying Moms to Stay Home: Short and Long Run Effects on Parents and Children. *SSRN Electronic Journal.* https://doi.org/10.2139/ssrn.4356214

71 Barschkett, M. (2022). Age-specific Effects of Early Daycare on Children's Health. *SSRN Electronic Journal.* https://doi.org/10.2139/ssrn.4304668

72 Cattan, S., Conti, G., Farquharson, C., Ginja, R., & Pecher, M. (n.d.). *Working paper*. Retrieved April 29, 2025, from https://ifs.org.uk/sites/default/files/2024-08/WP202243-The-health-effects-of-universal-early-childhood-interventions-evidence-from-Sure-Start%20%281%29.pdf

73 Bosque-Mercader, L. (2022). *The Effect of a Universal Preschool Programme on Long-Term Health Outcomes*. 2022.

Breivik, A.-L. (2020). Determinants of Health and Labor Market Outcomes : Three Essays in Applied Microeconomics. *Bora.uib.no*. https://doi.org/container/68/21/90/4b/6821904b-81b0-421e-8b35-557886a521a7

Ulferts, H., Wolf, K. M., & Anders, Y. (2019). Impact of Process Quality in Early Childhood Education and Care on Academic Outcomes: Longitudinal Meta-Analysis. *Child Development, 90*(5), 1474–1489. https://doi.org/10.1111/cdev.13296

Anders, J., Barr, A. C., & Smith, A. A. (2023). The Effect of Early Childhood Education on Adult Criminality: Evidence from the 1960s through 1990s. *American Economic Journal: Economic Policy, 15*(1), 37–69. https://doi.org/10.1257/pol.20200660

74 van Huizen, T., & Plantenga, J. (2018). Do children benefit from universal early childhood education and care? A meta-analysis of evidence from natural experiments. *Economics of Education Review, 66*(66), 206–222. https://doi.org/10.1016/j.econedurev.2018.08.001

75 Evans, D. K., Jakiela, P., & Amina Mendez Acosta. (2024). The Impacts of Childcare Interventions on Children's Outcomes in Low- and Middle-Income Countries: A Systematic Review. *AEA Papers and Proceedings, 114*, 463–466. https://doi.org/10.1257/pandp.20241015

76 Yamaguchi, S., Asai, Y., & Kambayashi, R. (2017). How Does Early Childcare Enrollment Affect Children, Parents, and Their Interactions? *SSRN Electronic Journal*. https://doi.org/10.2139/ssrn.2932875

77 Zachrisson, HD, et al. (2021). Universal Early Childhood Education and Care for Toddlers and Achievement Outcomes in Middle Childhood. *OSF Preprints*. https://doi.org/10.35542/osf.io/zrctw

78 Yazejian, N., Bryant, D., Freel, K., & Burchinal, M. (2015). High-quality early education: Age of entry and time in care differences in student outcomes for English-only and dual language learners. *Early Childhood Research Quarterly, 32*, 23–39. https://doi.org/10.1016/j.ecresq.2015.02.002

79 Atteberry, A., Bassok, D., & Wong, V. C. (2019). The Effects of Full-Day Prekindergarten: Experimental Evidence of Impacts on Children's School Readiness. *Educational Evaluation and Policy Analysis, 41*(4), 537–562. https://doi.org/10.3102/0162373719872197

80 Rey-Guerra, C., Zachrisson, H. D., Dearing, E., Berry, D., Kuger, S., Burchinal, M. R., Nærde, A., van Huizen, T., & Côté, S. M. (2022). Do more hours in center-based care cause more externalizing problems? A cross-national replication study. *Child Development, 94*(2), 458–477. https://doi.org/10.1111/cdev.13871

81 Cannon, J. S., Jacknowitz, A., & Painter, G. (2005). Is Full Better than Half? Examining the Longitudinal Effects of Full-Day Kindergarten Attendance. *SSRN Electronic Journal.* https://doi.org/10.2139/ssrn.755029

82 Friesen, J., Krauth, B., & Cohn, R. (2022). *The effect of universal full-day Kindergarten on student achievement.* https://www.sfu.ca/repec-econ/sfu/sfudps/dp22-01.pdf

83 Baker, M., Gruber, J., & Milligan, K. (2019). The Long-Run Impacts of a Universal Child Care Program. *American Economic Journal: Economic Policy, 11*(3), 1–26. https://doi.org/10.1257/pol.20170603

Baker, M., Gruber, J., & Milligan, K. (2008). Universal Child Care, Maternal Labor Supply, and Family Well-Being. *Journal of Political Economy, 116*(4), 709–745. https://doi.org/10.1086/591908

84 Ferguson, A., Gillett, C., Butler, B., & Sonnenschein, L. (2025, March 17). *Private childcare whistleblowers' disturbing experiences inside a sector putting profits before kids.* Abc.net.au; ABC News. https://www.abc.net.au/news/2025-03-17/private-childcare-centres-whistleblowers-abuse-four-corners/105058186

Ferguson, A., Sonnenschein, L., & Gillett, C. (2025, March 17). *Tens of thousands of children attend childcare centres that fail national standards.* Abc.net.au; ABC News. https://www.abc.net.au/news/2025-03-18/childcare-centres-regulation-quality-qualification-four-corners/105062514

85 NICHD Early Child Care Research Network. (2002). Early Child Care and Children's Development Prior to School Entry: Results from the NICHD Study of Early Child Care. *American Educational Research Journal, 39*(1), 133–164. https://doi.org/10.3102/00028312039001133

86 Nystad, K., Drugli, M. B., Stian Lydersen, Tveit, H. H., Ratib Lekhal, & Elisabet Solheim Buøen. (2024). Toddlers' Cortisol Levels in Childcare and at Home. *Early Education and Development*, 1–18. https://doi.org/10.1080/10409289.2024.2360873

87 Housman, D. K. (2017). The importance of emotional competence and self-regulation from birth: A case for the evidence-based emotional cognitive social early learning approach. *International Journal of Child Care and Education Policy, 11*(1). https://doi.org/10.1186/s40723-017-0038-6

88 Oliveira, P., & Fearon, P. (2019). The biological bases of attachment. *Adoption & Fostering, 43*(3), 274–293. https://doi.org/10.1177/0308575919867770

89 Chaudhary, N., Gül Deniz Salali, & Swanepoel, A. (2023). Sensitive responsiveness and multiple caregiving networks among Mbendjele BaYaka hunter-gatherers: Potential implications for psychological development and well-being. *Developmental Psychology*. https://doi.org/10.1037/dev0001601

90 Chaudhary, N., & Swanepoel, A. (2023). Editorial Perspective: What can we learn from hunter-gatherers about children's mental health? An evolutionary perspective. Journal of Child Psychology and Psychiatry, 64(10). https://doi.org/10.1111/jcpp.13773

91 Schore, A. N. (n.d.). Dr Allan. N. Schore. https://www.allanschore.com/

Wikipedia Contributors. (2024, November 1). *Penelope Leach*. Wikipedia; Wikimedia Foundation.

Belsky, J. (2001). Emanuel Miller Lecture Developmental Risks (Still) Associated with Early Child Care. *Journal of Child Psychology and Psychiatry, 42*(7), 845–859. https://doi.org/10.1111/1469-7610.00782

Barker, R. *The Incompatibility of Childcare for the Under-Threes*.

92 *Articles by Peter Cook - The Natural Child Project*. (2017). Naturalchild.org. https://www.naturalchild.org/articles/peter_cook/

93 Steve Biddulph. (n.d.). *Home.* www.stevebiddulph.com. https://www.stevebiddulph.com/Site_1/Home.html

94 Neufeld, G. (n.d.). *Neufeld Institute | Gordon Neufeld PhD.* Neufeld Institute. https://neufeldinstitute.org/

95 Australian Institute of Health and Welfare. (2015, September 30). *Literature review of the impact of early childhood education and care on learning and development, Summary.* Australian Institute of Health and Welfare. https://www.aihw.gov.au/reports/children-youth/learning-development-impact-of-early-childhood-edu/summary

96 *Productivity Commission - Access to Justice Arrangements report and recommendations.* (2025). Allens.com.au; Allens. https://www.allens.com.au/insights-news/insights/2014/12/productivity-commission---access-to-justice-arrangements

97 Vermeer, H. J., & van IJzendoorn, M. H. (2006). Children's elevated cortisol levels at daycare: A review and meta-analysis. *Early Childhood Research Quarterly, 21*(3), 390–401. https://doi.org/10.1016/j.ecresq.2006.07.004

98 Katz, D. A., Sprang, G., & Cooke, C. (2012). The Cost of Chronic Stress in Childhood: Understanding and Applying the Concept of Allostatic Load. *Psychodynamic Psychiatry, 40*(3), 469–480. https://doi.org/10.1521/pdps.2012.40.3.469

99 Evans, G. W., Kim, P., Ting, A. H., Tesher, H. B., & Shannis, D. (2007). Cumulative risk, maternal responsiveness, and allostatic load among young adolescents. *Developmental Psychology, 43*(2), 341–351. https://doi.org/10.1037/0012-1649.43.2.341

100 Duncan, G. J., Morris, P. A., & Rodrigues, C. (2011). Does money really matter? Estimating impacts of family income on young children's achievement with data from random-assignment experiments. *Developmental Psychology, 47*(5), 1263–1279. https://doi.org/10.1037/a0023875

CHAPTER ELEVEN

101 *Early childhood education and care sector and viability.* (2023). Aifs.gov.au. https://aifs.gov.au/research/research-snapshots/early-childhood-education-and-care-sector-and-viability

102 *Site Search | childcarecanada.org.* (n.d.). Childcarecanada.org. https://childcarecanada.org/sites/default/files/What%20research%20says%20about%20quality%20in%20fp%20np%20and%20p%20child%20care.pdf

103 Australian Institute of Health and Welfare. (2022). *Australia's children, early childhood education and care.* Australian Institute of Health and Welfare. https://www.aihw.gov.au/reports/children-youth/australias-children/contents/education/early-childhood-education

104 Tapscott, V. Take *Profit Motive out of Childcare, for Our Kids' Sake.* Theaustralian.com.au. www.theaustralian.com.au/commentary/take-profit-motive-out-of-childcare-for-our-kids-sake/news-story/91d9edae0fc918b7cd5a323f2091ec03.

105 Commission, A. C. and C. (2024, January 29). *December 2023 final report.* www.accc.gov.au. https://www.accc.gov.au/inquiries-and-consultations/childcare-inquiry-2023/december-2023-final-report

106 The Front Project. (2020, August 2). *ECEC History in Australia.* The Front Project. https://thefrontproject.org.au/about-us/history-of-ecec-in-australia

107 Professor Deborah Brennan. (2008, November 19). *Reassembling the childcare business • Inside Story.* Inside Story. https://insidestory.org.au/reassembling-the-childcare-business/

108 Manne, A. (2005). *Motherhood : how should we care for our children?* (p. 104). Allen & Unwin.

CHAPTER TWELVE

109 Manne, A. (2005). *Motherhood : how should we care for our children?* (p. 191). Allen & Unwin.

110 Education/Programs — *CoWork Crèche.* (2025). CoWork Crèche. CoWork Crèche. https://www.coworkcreche.com.au/educationprograms

111 *Why Being A Parent Is Good For Your Character.* Theaustralian.com.au. https://www.theaustralian.com.au/kamikaze-grannies-and-other-forces-of-nature

CHAPTER THIRTEEN

112 Zechner, M. (n.d.). *Childcare commons: Of feminist subversions of community and commune in Barcelona.* https://ephemerajournal.org/sites/default/files/2022-12/1%20Article_Zechner_%20Childcare%20commong.pdf

113 Sciarelli, R. (2024). Caring and commoning in political society: Insights from the Scugnizzo Liberato of Naples. *Urban Studies.* https://doi.org/10.1177/00420980231217375

CHAPTER FOURTEEN

114 Warren, E., & Amelia Warren Tyagi. (2004). *The two-income trap : why middle-class parents are going broke.* Basic Books.

115 Venker, S. (2017). *TWO-INCOME TRAP : why parents are choosing to stay home.* Permuted Press.

116 Tapscott, V. (2024). *Yacht envy, and the insidious curse of relative deprivation.* Theaustralian.com.au. https://www.theaustralian.com.au/inquirer/depression-envy-and-the-curse-of-comparing-your-life-to-others/news-story/c4c92861a29d6f30f93d8e1e9d40a4b0

117 Tapscott, V. (2023, September 27). *People think stay-at-home parents must be wealthy. But this is the true cost.* Mamamia. https://www.mamamia.com.au/single-income-family

118 *Defining Moments In The Erasure Of Womanhood.* Theaustralian.com.au. https://www.theaustralian.com.au/inquirer/women-win-the-mother-of-all-battles-on-the-home-front/news-story/6ec84927f21e17a008c06ff6568b73be

119 *Irish prime minister concedes defeat in a vote over constitutional amendments about family and women.* (2024, March 9). AP News. https://apnews.com/article/ireland-women-constitution-referendum-8eead7fd4ee13e76d77e8322bf348d0d

ABOUT THE AUTHOR

Virginia Tapscott

Virginia Tapscott is a mother of four children. She is a Founding Director of not-for-profit orgisation Parents Work Collective, an advocacy organisation that aims to shift the narratives around the importance of unpaid care work and advocates for more support for parents to have time to parent.

AUTHOR CONTACT

Email: vtapp62@gmail.com
Instagram: @virginia_tapscott

Acknowledgements

This book has been in the works since 2015. When my son was born I began writing compulsively about the experience of motherhood. Thank you to people who have read my work from the beginning and encouraged me to keep going. Even when I didn't hit the mark or my words were sloppy, people saw something in my work that they believed in. My readers constantly let me know when I am onto something important and have played an active role for the past decade in enabling me to crystallise and formulate the ideas in this book.

My family have had constant blind faith in me and supported me every step of the way. There is no way I could have written in this space to the extent that I have without them. Belief in ourselves can only get us so far. It is the belief that others have in us that gets us there in the end.

My kids have taught me so much. They are absolute wonders. They have been little champions in a situation that isn't always ideal. I would like to acknowledge the price they have paid in having a mother who got caught up in writing a book.

Projects like this are not just one person working late into the night. It is a collection of people, including my husband and my mum, who have put in the hard yards and made a sacrifice. I have written things that my whole family have had to carry. This hasn't been easy for them. They are often just as tired as me and they are such a big part in the victory of publication. I hope they know this.

Our Nanny Jess. A total gift. The only glue holding this show together some days. Thank you.

A photographer I worked with early on in my freelance career, Josh Smith, told me something I have never forgotten. One day we were out doing a story for R. M Williams Outback Magazine at a glorious farm near Barraba. It was a cracking sunny bluesky day doing the jobs we loved and getting paid for it. Outback Magazine remains one of the best paying publications I have worked for. It was a big break for me. Josh said, "If it was easy, everyone would be doing it."

I have often gone back to this moment in my mind, when things were tough. I'd like to thank Josh for letting a novice ride on his coat tails for a while.

In 2018 I wrote a book that I now recognise as what authors often refer to as the 'bottom drawer book'. This is a book we write to understand the process of writing a whole book while the content is likely not suitable for publication. Thanks to my husband and my mum for backing me with this book even though it will never see the light of day.

In 2019 when I was driving through the Warrumbungle's near Coonabarabran I received a call from the late Caroline Jones OA. I was the recipient of the Caroline Jones Rural Women in Media Award. To have such an accomplished and incredible woman support my work is one of the reasons I have been able to write this book. It was because of Caroline that I first made it onto the pages of The Australian. Emma MacDonald and the team at Women In Media remain one of the most positive and supportive organisations I have had the pleasure of being involved with.

I worked for Robin McConchie and Andrew Saunders, both legends in their own right at the national broadcaster. They taught me how to find the colour in a story and the angles that cut through. How to cut to the chase.

I have been edited by the best in the business. Ian and Wanda Dunnet at The Courier in Narrabri. Michelle Gunn, Jenny Campbell, Georgina Windsor and Claire Harvey at The Australian. Mark Muller at R. M. Williams Outback Magazine. Mia Freedman at Mamamia published my early criticisms of feminism when no other women's media would. They have been integral to the development of my voice as a writer. They taught me to write something that is impossible to refuse. Make it so people cannot look away. Editors know best.

In 2022 I tracked down Alannah Batho, a lawyer and mother based in Melbourne, who wrote a submission to the Work and Care Inquiry that I stumbled across. Her submission resonated strongly with me. It was the submission I would have liked to submit but lacked Alannah's skill in writing formal reports, organisation and literacy in navigating official government channels. I thought we would be a great team.

We decided to start a not-for-profit advocacy group, Parents Work Collective, in order to challenge policy and dominant narratives beyond writing about the issues in my columns. This organisation has been very effective and amassed a significant following, but we quickly realised we could not seriously challenge the prevailing discourse without some form of funding.

By 2023 I had a very untidy, half-cooked early draft of the current book. It needed a lot of work. I couldn't finish it alone. I sent a message to Alannah suggesting we try to publish the book with the proceeds going towards funding our work at Parents Work Collective. Alannah backed it whole heartedly but I couldn't find the drive and energy to finish the book. I knew there wasn't a heap of margin in selling books.

We decided on selling T-Shirts with the slogan 'All Mothers Work'. We were unbelievably excited to work with Phoebe Simmonds at The Memo who stocked our shirts. The merchandise was a sell-out, and this was our first funding. It was a crucial show of support from Phoebe and the broader community at a time when we were uncertain of what the future held for Parents Work Collective.

In 2024 we returned to the idea of publishing the book and crowdfunding it. Our board members, Jenny and Ishbel Cullen, also supported the idea and for that I am very thankful. Their involvement and belief in this work has been integral to our success.

It was around this time that Tara Shelton reached out to offer her help in growing our organisation. Without her advice, energy and creative drive this book would have remained in a word doc on my computer. Tara designed the original cover through her platform Motherism. To see the cover of the book, to see it as a real book, was the push I needed to turn my draft into the book.

We decided to use Kickstarter as the crowdfunding platform. We set the funding target at $33 000 and within 30 days we reached our target. We are forever grateful for the incredible generosity of our Kickstarter backers. You made this book happen.

I finished the book, but by mid 2025 I felt myself slipping. I became unable to edit it or proofread what I had written. With the finish line in sight I felt like I just couldn't get there. I was unable to make decisions and market it. When it came to the arduous process of proof reading, multiple passes, decision making and final edits I relied heavily on Alannah to do this work. Without Alannah this book would not have happened.

Alannah is an incredible mother and professional. I can't believe how lucky I am to work with her. When Parents Work Collective was invited to a hearing with the Productivity Commission regarding our submission to the Inquiry into Universal Childcare I will never forget Alannah's clarity and her poise. In that setting, face-to-face and not hiding behind a keyboard, I really faltered. Alannah shone. Her commitment to this movement has been unwavering and constant. She does thankless, at times boring, behind-the-scenes work and I really want that acknowledged. Everyone needs an Alannah, but she is an incredibly rare find.

A huge thanks also to our broader Parents Work Collective community, popping up in our DMs and emails with words of encouragement or helpful information.

Thanks to Amanda Spedding, Sophie White and Julie Postance of iinspire media who also helped get this book to publication with incredible skill and know how. Thanks to Parnell Palme McGuinness and Veronika Winkels for your testimonials. It still doesn't feel real.

www.ingramcontent.com/pod-product-compliance
Lightning Source LLC
Chambersburg PA
CBHW050550160426
43199CB00015B/2598